T0110708

Cambridge Elements ≡

edited by
Samantha Rayner
University College London
Leah Tether
University of Bristol

READING COMPUTER-GENERATED TEXTS

Leah Henrickson
University of Leeds

CAMBRIDGE
UNIVERSITY PRESS

CAMBRIDGE
UNIVERSITY PRESS

University Printing House, Cambridge CB2 8BS, United Kingdom

One Liberty Plaza, 20th Floor, New York, NY 10006, USA

477 Williamstown Road, Port Melbourne, VIC 3207, Australia

314–321, 3rd Floor, Plot 3, Splendor Forum, Jasola District Centre,
New Delhi – 110025, India

79 Anson Road, #06–04/06, Singapore 079906

Cambridge University Press is part of the University of Cambridge.

It furthers the University's mission by disseminating knowledge in the pursuit of
education, learning, and research at the highest international levels of excellence.

www.cambridge.org
Information on this title: www.cambridge.org/9781108822862
DOI: 10.1017/9781108906463

First published 2021

A catalogue record for this publication is available from the British Library.

ISBN 978-1-108-82286-2 Paperback
ISSN 2514-8524 (online)
ISSN 2514-8516 (print)

Reading Computer-Generated Texts

Elements in Publishing and Book Culture

DOI: 10.1017/9781108906463
First published online: January 2021

Leah Henrickson
University of Leeds
Author for correspondence: Leah Henrickson, L.R.Henrickson@leeds.ac.uk

ABSTRACT: Natural language generation (NLG) is the process wherein computers produce output in readable human languages. Such output takes many forms, including news articles, sports reports, prose fiction, and poetry. These computer-generated texts are often indistinguishable from human-written texts, and they are increasingly prevalent. NLG is here, and it is everywhere. However, readers are often unaware that what they are reading has been computer-generated. This Element considers how NLG conforms to and confronts traditional understandings of authorship and what it means to be a reader. It argues that conventional conceptions of authorship, as well as of reader responsibility, change in instances of NLG. What is the social value of a computer-generated text? What does NLG mean for modern writing, publishing, and reading practices? Can an NLG system be considered an author? This Element explores such questions, while presenting a theoretical basis for future studies.

KEYWORDS: natural language generation, computer-generated texts, reader response, authorship, digital humanities

ISBNs: 9781108822862 (PB), 9781108906463 (OC)
ISSNs: 2514–8524 (online), 2514–8516 (print)

Contents

1 Introduction

Every morning, Simon walks down the street to his local café in Wolverhampton. He orders a medium black filter coffee, which he nurses as he flips through the *Express & Star*, an independent regional newspaper. First, the cover story. Then, the less pressing items. The newspaper's contributors are good at what they do, tending towards fair representation of issues and citing relevant supporting data. Today, a story entitled 'Majority of New Mothers in Wolverhampton Are Unmarried' catches Simon's eye. He reads the story's introduction: 'The latest figures reveal that 56.5 per cent of the 3,476 babies born across the area in 2016 have parents who were not married or in a civil partnership when the birth was registered. That's a slight increase on the previous year.' *This is a sensitive issue*, thinks Simon. *Well, it takes a special kind of journalist to consider such a subject so objectively.* Simon continues reading the article, which cites figures and statements courtesy of the Office for National Statistics. It is not until he reaches the end of the text that Simon reads the following statement: 'This article has been computer-generated by Urbs Media, crafting stories and harnessing automation to mass localise.'

Simon looks up from the paper, quickly setting it down onto the table in front of him. He does not know what to think about a computer-generated news article. *You read things to connect to other people's stories*, he ponders. *If a computer writes a story, you take away that human connection. But here, there's no criticism, there's no opinion. I suppose it's so factual that I don't really mind if this article is computer-generated or human-generated.* Simon still does not know how he feels about computer-generated texts. The only certainty: *Now I feel like I'm on the set of a sci-fi film.*

This anecdote is fictitious but the technology is most certainly not. The 'unmarried mothers' article (Anon., 2017) appeared on the *Express & Star*'s website on 29 November 2017, as countless more computer-generated articles appeared in other news outlets worldwide that same day. However, most of these articles (including those by Urbs Media) actually do not include any disclaimers about their production processes. 'Crafting stories and harnessing automation to mass localise' is a slogan that Urbs uses to describe its service on the company's website

(Urbs Media, n.d.), but it does not accompany any of their articles. Moreover, Simon's conflicted feelings have been paraphrased from a series of focus groups conducted to discern readers' emotional responses to the idea of computer-generated texts (Henrickson, 2019c). While some may regard a computer's ability to generate intelligible narratives as being contained within the realm of science fiction, the technology that enables a computer to generate cogent prose has been in development for more than half a century. Computer scientists have long been engaged with programming computers to generate texts that are indistinguishable from those written by humans. Now we have reached a point when there are systems generating texts that we may read as part of our daily routines, unaware of their being computer-generated. The production of data-driven sport, weather, election, and business intelligence reports has been assigned to computers capable of producing these texts at a rate incomparable to that of humans, and on personalised scales that could hardly be considered efficient uses of time for paid human labour. Yet when we read these texts, we assume that they are social products, the results of human thought and intention, rather than computer-generated.

This is natural language generation (NLG). NLG is the computational production of textual output in everyday human languages. NLG systems are increasingly prevalent in our modern digital climate, as we have seen the emergence of numerous companies that specialise in generating output intended for mass readerships and readerships of one alike. Yseop works with an international insurance company to provide personalised explanations of refusals or partial agreements of credit insurance allocations (Anon., 2019). Phrasee generates marketing copy aligned with its many partners' unique brand voices (Malm, 2020). Narrative Science has worked in partnership with Deloitte to generate client-friendly narrative reports related to such issues as budget optimisation, financial operations, and internal auditing (Krittman, Matthews, and Glascott, 2015). These are only a few examples of NLG's current applications as implemented by a burgeoning industry based around this technology. Anyone who reads data-driven news has likely encountered at least one computer-generated text, perhaps unknowingly. Computer-generated texts are both online and in print, and they are everywhere.

This Element offers an introduction to the social and literary implications of NLG from a humanities perspective. More specifically, it examines how computer-generated texts challenge conventional understandings of authorship and what it means to be a reader. Accentuating the humanities perspective employed, this Element refers to NLG as 'algorithmic authorship', save for in discussions of NLG's technical functionality and in quotations. It should be noted that 'algorithmic authorship' is not a term coined for this Element. Some (generally popular) articles have used the term, but it has largely gone unused by NLG developers. This lack of widespread use may reflect the current emphasis on system development over output reception, for the term draws attention to the nuances of authorship as it applies to human writers and NLG systems. The use of 'algorithmic authorship' therefore distinguishes this Element's sociological focus from a process-focused computer science perspective: NLG is the technology; algorithmic authorship is the concept. While NLG refers to the process of text production, 'algorithmic authorship' more clearly refers to the social players – and the relevant sociocultural circumstances – involved in this technology's applications. 'Algorithmic authorship' situates NLG systems within the complex history of authorship – a history driven by both human and non-human agents – that is explored here.

NLG systems produce a wide range of texts for pragmatic and aesthetic purposes. News items, image and video descriptions, and prose fiction are just some examples of NLG's current applications. This Element focuses primarily on English-language prose texts for human readers, including works that are expository (e.g. news and business reports) and aesthetic (e.g. stories). The computer-generated texts cited in this Element exist in static and linear reading forms. Interactive applications of NLG – for example, chatbots – warrant their own analyses, and are thus only referred to when contextually necessary. Likewise, those computer-generated texts produced for reading by machines rather than humans – for example, content generated to promote Web traffic through search engine optimisation – are outside of this Element's scope, but have already been investigated elsewhere. Further, I do not deny the importance of genre differences in literary criticism, or wish to discredit readers' genre-specific expectations; expository and aesthetic texts prompt different reading practices and interpretive processes, as do texts of different genres. However, the focus of this Element is not one of literary analysis, but of readers' responses to the very concept of NLG itself. Once the stage has been set by such general research, future studies are better positioned to conduct genre-specific analyses. For now, concentration on textual output actually detracts from the more fundamental issue of determining NLG's unique contributions to the modern textual landscape: a landscape permeated with varied modes of human–computer collaboration. Without recognition of these contributions, one cannot fully appreciate the roles of NLG systems as cultural artefacts, as reflections of contemporary social values and needs, and in turn as re-enforcers or interrogators of these values and needs.

Of course, an NLG system's output must at least somewhat conform to readers' expectations of literary convention for that output and system to be relevant. Complete narratives comprise a beginning, a middle, and an end; genre conventions are anticipated; every text has an author. Indeed, it is not unreasonable to assume that a text reflects human agency, and that a text – regardless of genre – is an effort to communicate a predetermined message. With this assumption, readers engage their interpretive faculties to assign authorial intention, developing a perceived contract with the author. I refer to this author–reader contract as 'the hermeneutic contract' (Henrickson, 2018a). The establishment of an author–reader contract is warranted given the underlying assumption that through language we articulate and legitimise lived experiences to ourselves and others. Our perceptions of the world, and others' perceptions of ourselves, are shaped and shared by the words at our disposal. It is through language that agency is exercised, and that potentialities are realised. The hermeneutic contract is therefore rooted in an expectation of agency informed by lived experience.

Computer-generated texts in their current state complicate the hermeneutic contract. The hermeneutic contract rests on two assumptions: that readers believe that authors want readers to be interested in their texts, and that authors want readers to understand their texts. Even in instances of the avant-garde, authors are still presumed to have produced their texts with some sort of communicative intention that justifies unintelligibility; a reader's willingness to accept such writing as intentionally incomprehensible is for that reader to fulfil the hermeneutic contract. Ultimately, the hermeneutic contract supposes intelligibility for hypothetical readers who are able to engage with the social and literary conventions employed by what Tereza Pavlíčková (2013) calls the 'imagined author', in a nod to Wayne Booth's (1961) 'implied author'. The imagined author matters, Pavlíčková explains in a later paper with Ranjana Das (Das and Pavlíčková, 2013: 393), because its presence contributes to a reader's sense of familiarity with the writing subject, in turn helping to determine the reader's trust in a text's source. But what happens when the human author appears to be removed, and agency and intention may not be readily identifiable? The author of a computer-generated text is often an obscured figure, an uncertain entanglement of human and computer. With an eye to cultural vacillation, this Element offers a unique interdisciplinary consideration of a technology – NLG – that has been under development for more than half a century, but which has not yet been subject to any substantial analysis from a humanities perspective. Drawing from book history, media studies, computer science, digital humanities, and the social sciences, this Element offers a peek into the kaleidoscopic state of the art.

Section 2 – 'Discovering Natural Language Generation' – presents a technical introduction to NLG, defining technical terms as they are used within this Element: algorithm, program, system, and machine learning. It reviews the functionalities of some historical and modern NLG systems, as well as the history of systematised writing more generally. This section provides the necessary context for determining whether readers' perceptions of computational capability and expectations of system functionality are justified. Section 3 – 'The Development of Authorship' – offers a theoretical examination into which aspects of modern social life algorithmic authorship manifest and mobilise, arguing that algorithmic authorship reflects a current tendency towards individualisation. Section 4 – 'Algorithmic Authorship and Agency' – suggests a semantic shift from considering NLG systems as tools for actualising human ideation to NLG systems as social agents – and authors – in themselves. Such a semantic shift permits a more reflective discussion about the transformative power of these systems' output, explicitly recognising their distinct social contributions. Having presented a framework for reading computer-generated texts, this Element concludes with recommendations for further studies.

2 Discovering Natural Language Generation

2.1 Introduction

The year is 1845. Spectators gather in Piccadilly's Egyptian Hall, eagerly anticipating a demonstration of John Clark's Eureka machine. With the mere pull of a lever, the Eureka generates a grammatically and metrically correct line of Latin dactylic hexameter. For the price of one shilling, visitors witness the mechanised spectacle of the wooden, bureau-like contraption moving its wooden staves, metal wires, and revolving drums to produce a line of Latin verse that appears in the machine's front window. While each line adheres to a predefined system of scansion and strict syntactic formula – adjective | noun | adverb | verb | noun | adjective – the Eureka can churn out an estimated 26 million permutations (Hall, 2007: 227). Eureka! Mechanised text production is in the spotlight.

Not everyone was excited. An item in the 'Miscellanea' section of *The Athenæum*'s June 1845 issue (Anon., 1845) notes that Clark had worked on the machine for thirteen years 'as it would seem from the mere sport of the thing, and in a spirit of indifference as to what might be its subsequent use. ... I do not see its immediate utility.' Other contemporary critics too expressed scepticism: one reviewer (Anon., 1846: 133) deemed the machine a 'useless toy', while another (Nuttall, 1845: 140) asserted that it was 'little better than a mere puzzle, which any school-boy might perform by a simpler process.' Modern scholar Jason David Hall (2007: 228), however, has described the machine as 'much more than a show-place diversion: this kitsch device – at once the technological embodiment of and a parody of Victorian prosodic science [the study of verse and meter] – was a literally interactive discursive site, the focus of a popular prosodic discourse that existed alongside institutional debates.' Hall sees the Eureka as a meeting place between those of academe and members of the general public (who could spare the shilling required to enter the exhibition). Indeed, the machine was a 'material embodiment ... of the institutional practice of Victorian prosody' that spoke to academics and amateurs alike (Hall, 2007: 234). According to Hall, the Eureka evoked curiosity in various publics at the onset of the golden age of automata: machines programmed to operate on their own, often imitating the actions of humans or animals. Mechanised writing seemed especially enticing, with some American and British newspapers reporting on (fictitious) writing machines that tended towards producing poetry (Anon., 1841a; Anon., 1841b; Anon., 1844).[1] The Eureka serves as an early tangible example of mechanised writing's long-standing appeal to mass curiosity.

Technically, the Eureka was primitive; it just randomly applied words in accordance with strict programmed constraints. 'All it really did,' Jason David Hall (2017: 130) explains, 'was combine a limited array of integers, uniting predictability (all values were determined beforehand) with unpredictability (the order in which the values might be arranged was not).' However, the enthusiasm garnered for the Eureka's mechanised production of verse speaks not just to the Victorians' fascination with automata, but also to a continued enchantment with technological capability. The Eureka seems more a mechanical toy than any convincing form of autonomy, a bibelot rather than a bard. Nevertheless, recent efforts to restore the machine (Eureka AHRC Project, n.d.) perpetuate the sense of curiosity about a technology that helped pave the way for what we now call NLG.

NLG enjoyed a surge of interest within the academic community throughout the 1970s to 1990s. This interest also permeated the popular sphere. In 1986, Arthur C. Clarke (2000) published a fictional short story about 'The Steam-Powered Word Processor', which Reverend Charles Cabbage uses to mindlessly produce his sermons. Even earlier, in 1954, Roald Dahl wrote about 'The Great Automatic Grammatisator': a novel-producing machine that one Adolph Knipe uses to render human writers obsolete. Despite such widespread interest, though, NLG research has only recently begun engendering distinct intellectual traditions, especially related to developmental approaches. As David McDonald (1986: 12) suggests, this may be a result of the individualised nature of systems. Indeed, few NLG systems comprising the field's lineage remain. Written in programming languages now extinct, or saved in digital formats that have deteriorated or disappeared altogether, many of these systems survive only through secondary literature. Further, developers tend not to build upon

---

[1] Thanks to James Ryan for his digital curation of these materials.

work that has already been done, perhaps for reasons of inadequate digital preservation and / or claims for intellectual property. The field is in disarray, with no comprehensive analysis of NLG output reception ever having been published. As a result, we do not know where computer-generated texts fit within our current conceptions of authorship and reading. This section offers the necessary technical context for succeeding sections, which examine where computer-generated texts fit within conventional understandings of authorship and what it means to be a reader as per the hermeneutic contract.

2.2 Technical Terminology

Preceding any substantial analysis of NLG, numerous technological terms must be defined. This is, as any etymologist might anticipate, not so easily done. Despite technological terms like 'program' and 'algorithm' seeping into common speech, the meanings of these words as characterised by historical and current usage are hardly stable or precise. The definitions provided here are working definitions for this Element and should not be considered comprehensive or static. Technological developments force alterations of all of these terms – alterations that are hardly consistent across fields of study. Rather than offer conclusive definitions, the following paragraphs simply offer semantic scrutiny that informs the following discussion.

Colloquial understandings of algorithms often synonymise them with computer programs. However, these terms are not synonymous. Using a programming language (e.g. Java or C++), a program executes a set of instructions provided by a developer to solve a problem through fulfilment of a predetermined task. Each of these instructions is an algorithm. A program may comprise just one algorithm, or it may comprise a series of algorithms. An algorithm is a function with at least one defined source of input that produces a defined output. In some cases, the defined output may be an instruction to refer to another algorithm. In all cases, algorithms must be unambiguously specific. This is demonstrated by an activity popular with Introduction to Computer Science teachers, during which students direct the teacher to make a peanut butter and jelly sandwich. When a student tells the teacher to 'put the jelly on the bread' (an instruction), the teacher may then dunk her hand into the jelly jar and messily slop the jelly onto the loaf.

The student must instead direct the teacher to 'grip the knife's handle with your right hand', and then to 'move your right hand, still gripping the knife, up approximately seven inches', and so on. Each of these instructions represents an algorithm. Recipe analogies are commonly used when clarifying what an algorithm is. One extra teaspoon of baking powder can collapse a cake.

This Element, however, refers to NLG *systems* rather than programs. This is because generated output more often results from a series of programs than from a single program. Each program informs the next program's functionality, and together these programs make a system.

But all aspects of a system may not remain static. There are, after all, numerous problems that cannot be solved with fixed input data, instead necessitating an ever-growing and/or unstable corpus. In these instances, machine learning algorithms are more suitable. Search engines employ learning algorithms to navigate the Web and provide more relevant results in a digital landscape constantly altered by the daily emergence of countless new websites. News platforms employ learning algorithms to summarise current events by drawing from myriad articles and social media posts. A machine learning system has by necessity achieved a sort of autopoiesis, capable of maintaining itself through a network of processes that ensures the system's continuous production, maintenance, and improvement. A machine learning system could be viewed as a small technological ecosystem, with limited autonomy within its specified domain. As its algorithms evolve in response to a sort of lived experience, the system becomes increasingly independent of its creator.

Given the semantic, grammatical, and syntactic complexities of natural language, inputting all of a language's rules (and exceptions) into an NLG system would be a daunting task for even the most skilled linguist. What is more, by the time all the rules had been inputted, the linguistic landscape would have changed. For these reasons, many new NLG systems employ unsupervised machine learning, which applies inductive logic associated with unlabelled data by using clustering and association techniques to detect patterns that humans might overlook. Rather than teach a system a language, a developer may instead teach the system *how to learn* language, thereby allowing it to update its vocabulary, grammar, and syntax according to actual contemporary usage. Tang et al. (2016: 2) identify two approaches to NLG: rule- or template-based approaches and machine learning approaches, with the latter now often employing recurrent neural networks (RNNs). Many historical systems have tended towards the former. A recent example of the latter approach comes from a team at Google Brain. In preliminary tests, the team's RNN used unsupervised machine learning to distinguish linguistic patterns across approximately 12,000 (mostly fiction) e-books, amounting to approximately 80 million sentences, from the English Google Books Corpora (Bowman et al., 2016). Instead of constructing sentences one word at a time through next-step predictions (e.g. through Markov chains, which use statistical probabilities to generate texts word by word), Google Brain's system can construct sentences in more complex ways that accommodate global concepts and 'big idea' conveyance, resulting in output that better mimics human writing styles. In another recent example, Microsoft's Twitterbot Tay (@TayandYou), 'a chatbot created for 18- to 24- year-olds in the U.S. for entertainment purposes,' likewise mimicked human writing styles (Lee, 2016). However, those writing styles – applied by Twitter users interacting with Tay – led to the bot's spouting lewd and racially charged remarks within hours. Tay was promptly deactivated and Microsoft issued a formal apology.

The Tay fiasco shows that, in any machine learning system, a developer must in some way specify what the system is intended to do, and must embed algorithmic preferences and constraints to ensure that the system aligns with its intended purpose. 'If the rules of legal chess are not built into a chess-playing machine as constraints, and if the machine is given the power to learn, it may change without notice from a chess-playing machine into a machine doing a totally different task,' Norbert Wiener warns in his 1950 *The Human Use of Human Beings* (205–6). 'On the other hand, a chess-playing machine with the rules built in as constraints may still be a learning machine as to tactics and policies.' Tay serves as just one modern affirmation of the need for constraints in machine learning NLG systems. With no moral bounds and limited programmed appreciation for the nuances of language, Tay was unable to avoid offence. Tay's computational capacity for creation was insufficiently curbed.

2.3 Historically Salient NLG Systems

Some of the earliest forms of NLG were interactive systems that depended upon human users inputting comments in natural languages to receive computer-generated natural language responses. While seemingly simple, these responses stemmed from significant technological developments within natural language processing. Such systems, however, could hardly be considered autonomous or capable of independent communicative intention. Their output was predictable, determined by regular user feedback. Only two conversational systems are noted here, but such systems – now called chatbots – continue to be developed extensively today (Natale, in press).

ELIZA was an early chatbot developed by MIT's Joseph Weizenbaum from 1964 to 1966. The system adopted multiple personae through various sets of scripts that searched for keywords and then repurposed these keywords according to programmed rules (Weizenbaum, 1966: 37–42). DOCTOR, the system's most well-known script, transformed ELIZA into a Rogerian psychotherapist. In this script, ELIZA remodelled users' inputted statements into open-ended questions that prompted users to input more details that continued the conversational cycle. ELIZA's output was determined by user input, and the system's perspective was tailored to the human individual commanding the conversation. Users felt understood because the system adopted their own language to craft its open-ended prompts for elaboration, repeating what had been said with only slight alterations to syntactic form. Without the user to guide the conversation, ELIZA was rendered mute and moot.

In the wake of ELIZA's success, Terry Winograd developed SHRDLU between 1968 and 1970 for his doctoral thesis, which was completed within the same MIT lab with which Joseph Weizenbaum was affiliated. SHRDLU's name refers to 'ETAOIN SHRDLU', a phrase that hot metal type-casters could easily use to fill space in faulty lines of type because these letters comprised the first two columns of their keyboards. Although SHRDLU's name nods to its linguistic ability, it did not generate language on its own, but demonstrated natural language understanding using a computer-simulated scene comprising a table, a 'hand' (like a virtual claw from an arcade grabber machine), a box, and several blocks and pyramids of different sizes and colours. It executed commands, answered questions, and prompted users to provide further information if needed. SHRDLU was significant not only because it could interact with its users by processing English-language input and responding appropriately, but also because it had a memory of sorts. For example, the system could remember that Winograd had defined a 'steeple' as a structure that contains two green cubes and a pyramid (Winograd, 1971: 52–5). SHRDLU could also correctly answer questions about actions it had executed in the past, demonstrating a primitive – however mechanical – lived experience.

While Winograd did not explicitly intend SHRDLU to be a work of interactive fiction, Professor of Digital Media Nick Montfort deems SHRDLU 'the first work with all the formal elements of interactive fiction.' According to Montfort (2005: 85), SHRDLU 'allowed for more interesting potential narratives, simulated spaces, and challenges to later be integrated with the sort of structure it exemplified. By augmenting SHRDLU's parser and world model (actually, a far simplified version of these) in this way, interactive fiction could be fully realized.' SHRDLU was a precursor to NLG as we now know it: a field that still necessarily depends upon human–computer interaction despite increasing computational autonomy. The systems described below exemplify numerous forms such interplay has taken.

Early systems like ELIZA and SHRDLU contributed to widespread enthusiasm for computational language use that spurred developments in NLG. Within only a few years, NLG systems that generated texts longer than just a few lines, and with cohesive narrative elements, were steadily being created worldwide.

Research indicates that the earliest prose generation systems emerged throughout the 1950s and 1960s (Montfort and Fedorova, 2012: 82–3; Roberts, 2017; Ryan, 2017). However, Sheldon Klein et al.'s automatic novel writer (otherwise unnamed) is widely recognised as the first narrative NLG system. This novel writer was capable of generating 2,100-word murder-mystery stories 'with semantic deep structure' in less than 19 seconds. A 1973 University of Wisconsin technical report (Klein et al., 1973: 1) touts this system as 'part of an automated linguistic tool so powerful and of such methodological significance that we are compelled to claim a major breakthrough in linguistic

and computational linguistic research.' The automatic novel writer oper-
ated under heavy constraint, though, and its output was predictable.
Reflecting the literary objectives of its developers and users, six potential
plots were predetermined by programmed templates, and a story's character specifications were inputted by system users through numerical
valuation of specific traits. The system generated its stories as per murder
mystery scripts: preset sequences of actions that dictated characters'
interactions within a typical murder mystery story world. Like a child
learning the intricacies of fiction, the system generated only simple
sentences comprising one independent clause each, and only within the
story domain of murder mysteries. Yet the most significant result of the
system's development was not so much its output as its influence on the
development of the most prominent early narrative NLG system: TALE-
SPIN. The automatic novel writer's strict adherence to coded templates
would never allow for nuanced story characters and worlds. The system's
output included 'nothing that says what people need, nothing that says
why people make the decisions they do, nothing that explains people's
reactions to one another, nothing that represents the complexities of the
physical world. The purpose of TALE-SPIN is to address exactly these
issues' (Meehan, 1976: 9).

TALE-SPIN was developed by James Meehan from 1975 to 1977 for
a Yale doctorate. The system generated stories resembling Aesopian fables
centred on the lives of anthropomorphised animals. Meehan described TALE-
SPIN as a goal-directed problem-solving system that used virtual blueprints to
construct story worlds according to a user's selections from lists of character
and plot specifications. Although Meehan intended for TALE-SPIN to simulate human thought processes, the system could hardly be said to have
possessed any capacity for self-reflexivity (Meehan, 1976: 4–5). Meehan
(1976: 107) himself described TALE-SPIN as 'a simulator of the real world:
Turn it on and watch all the people. The purpose of the simulator is to model
rational behavior; the people in it are supposed to act like real people. To do
that, we have to model various kinds of human thinking, how people relate to
each other socially, for example.' Yet TALE-SPIN did not create an entire
world at once, wherein characters could move freely, but constructed its
microworlds in light of the current protagonist's goals, revealing only what

was necessary for the story's completion. Moreover, TALE-SPIN generated its stories using three modes, all of which were heavily dependent upon user direction (Meehan, 1976: 15–17). The user and system were co-creators, as it was the user who decided characters and relationships, as well as plot directions and details. TALE-SPIN did not simulate human thought; its stories were manifestations of human intention. TALE-SPIN, however, used its own language to generate stories in its own authorial voice, strengthening the illusion of computational self-sufficiency and agency.

Succeeding systems were developed in explicit response to TALE-SPIN, as were AUTHOR (Dehn, 1989) and MINSTREL (Turner, 1993), or at least nodded to their distinguished ancestor, as did UNIVERSE (Lebowitz, 1985) and GRANDMOTHER (Casebourne, 1996). Outside of the academy, William Chamberlain and Thomas Etter developed Racter, which generated what was advertised as 'the first book ever written by a computer': *The Policeman's Beard Is Half Constructed* (Racter [Chamberlain and Etter], 1984). Collegiate or civil, all of these systems reflect individualised – and short-lived – efforts, and represent various developmental approaches and aims. They are laden with human values, and are all human-controlled, albeit within varying contexts of design and power. All were programmed to generate output that resembled typical forms of human-written texts and/or mimicked human writers' cognitive processes during text production: namely, those processes associated with problem solving and creativity. Some systems were developed to facilitate reflection upon human creativity through the systematisation of cognitive processes associated with acts of creation; others were developed to model human cognition, revealing that human thought processes associated with acts of writing are too complex to mechanise entirely, but seemingly straightforward enough to justify attempts to do so anyway. The only one of these systems developed outside of an academic context – Racter – emerged as an exploration of novelty, an ode to literary wackiness. Whether for experimentation or entertainment, all of these systems have served as means of exploring the theoretical and practical facets of creativity as it is applied to authorship of cohesive narratives. They were born out of the interconnectedness of humans and their technologies, and driven by curiosity about computational competence as embodied by NLG, conscious or coded.

2.4 Systematised Writing

To meaningfully communicate requires awareness of the self, and of the self in relation to surrounding circumstances. NLG systems cannot (yet) be said to possess such awareness, but many have *appeared* to. Although some systems have practised programmed self-evaluation that may be seen as mimicking human writers' non-linear writing processes, these evaluations have only validated the originality of generated stories in relation to past output. While developments in machine learning may lead – are leading – to the creation of NLG systems that are able to autonomously situate themselves within a variety of social contexts, so long as systems depend upon human participation in text generation through, for example, determination of plot points and character profiles, these systems can never truly practise any behaviour of thought or creativity equivalent to that of humans.

Yet the output from these systems is not wholly distinct from human-written texts. Like the experimental writers of the 1960s, for example, NLG systems depend upon the systemisation of language according to predetermined rules that reflect communicative and aesthetic intentions. As per the Oulipo group's extended name – Ouvroir de littérature potentielle (workshop of potential literature) – potentialities of language and meaning are explored through the conscious application of constraint. An Oulipian work is produced less from the intention to convey a particular message and more from the intention to discover new worlds of syntactic and semantic possibility by applying strict linguistic constraints. Jean Lescure's (1973) N+7 (S+7 in French) procedure, for example, replaces every noun in a human-written text with the seventh one listed after it in a dictionary. In this way, the human-written text is altered to create a new text using the same syntactic formula but resulting in a different semantic meaning. Readers are tasked with interpreting Oulipian texts that may seem nonsensical at first glance, with translating their gibberish into significance. For a more playful alternative, one need only look to the popular fill-in-the-blanks word game Mad Libs. In Mad Libs, players complete a story template that they themselves cannot read by suggesting words with specified narrative functions (e.g. noun, verb). The story is then read aloud, with hilarity usually ensuing. An NLG system operates similarly, selecting messages to convey in its output, as well as appropriate words for conveying these messages. Even for the generation of non-fiction reports – seemingly objective narratives emerging from textual or numerical data – an NLG system engages in an aesthetic exercise of word selection to ensure that its output is both interesting and understandable. Moreover, like an Oulipian or Mad Libs text, part of the computer-generated text's attraction is the novelty of its production, and its occasional deviation from expected authorial comprehensibility.

But it is not just word choice that may be systematised; structural models of literature are no recent development. William Wallace Cook's 1928 *Plotto*, including more than 1,000 short plot outlines for aspiring authors, is just one early example of a writing tool that operated on the basis of systematised language and story structure. Georges Polti's 1895 *Thirty-Six Dramatic Situations*, which suggested fewer plot outlines, is an even earlier example. Wycliffe Hill similarly schematised plots in his 1919 *Ten Million Photoplay Plots*, and later claimed to have invented a 'Plot Robot' that generated hundreds of plots across various genres of fiction (Anon., 2010). Centuries prior, by no later than 1677, one John Peter published a book including tables for 'artificial versifying | a new way to make Latin verses'. NLG systems evidently do not represent the onset of narrative systematisation, but rather extend a lineage of such practice into computational contexts.

2.5 Conclusion

And here we find ourselves, following a history of mechanised text production beginning in 1845, but still uncertain as to where this technology fits within our modern age. Just as with the Eureka's spectators, modern readers are usually offered little more than an NLG system's surface realisations. A system's constraints, determined by human developers, are indistinguishable, hidden within a black box of code that may never be shared, perhaps due to intellectual property protection or patent limitations. Developers may therefore capitalise on humans' long-standing fascination with mechanised text production, as well as on each individual user's instinct to fill in a text's conceptual gaps. Development continues, but we still do not know where computer-generated texts fit within our current conceptions of authorship and what it means to be a reader. We have yet to fully discover NLG and all that it entails.

NLG systems are still far from achieving the autonomy that one assumes of a human writer, despite developers' efforts. Human involvement is integral to the creation, maintenance, and operation of these systems. However, this involvement is rarely overt. As a result, understanding where NLG systems fit within the conventional hermeneutic contract that drives modern reading experiences is hardly straightforward. What does authorship as a concept mean in instances of computer-generated texts? How is the reader expected to respond to one of these texts? Who – or what – is the author? The next two sections consider such questions.

3 The Development of Authorship

3.1 Introduction

In 2012, one Amazon customer (Smiggy) enthusiastically reviewed an unusual book. 'This is an epic tale that rises to Orwellian heights of greatness and is certainly nothing to be sneezed at,' the reviewer raved. 'A truly riveting read from cover to cover with a real snorter of a twist near the end (no spoilers). If it was possible to rate this six stars on Amazon then I would, I highly recommend even despite me having to save up for a few months to afford this!' What was this book? *The 2007 Report on Facial Tissue Stock Excluding Toweling, Napkin, and Toilet Paper: World Market Segmentation by City*, by Professor Philip M. Parker, Ph.D. (2006a), available in paperback for a mere £795.

Philip Parker is not an author in the typical sense of the word. He is a computer programmer, and *The 2007 Report on Facial Tissue Stock* is one of his thousands of computer-generated books. Parker has patented a set of algorithms to generate, market, and distribute physical codices whose texts adhere to highly formulaic templates. These are often market reports and reference materials, generated to meet the needs of underserved communities such as those with niche interests, or even those whose languages have a limited number of native speakers. Parker's patent application ('Method and Apparatus for Automated Authoring and Marketing' (US 7266767 B2), 2006) touts his method of text production as a means for combatting the financial and labour pressures of traditional publishing, such as the costs and management of authors and editors. The patent application also notes the method as preventing human error throughout production, and boasts greater economic profitability than traditional human authorship by using extant print-on-demand systems, and by eliminating the need to employ humans to write highly formulaic and repetitive texts.

Parker's generated texts demonstrate the potential to fulfil niche demands for which mass production would not be economically viable. Parker's generation system has been administered through ICON Group International (n.d.), which sells such specialised global market research reports as the 176-page *2007–2012 Outlook for Instant Chocolate Milk,*

Weight Control Products, Whole Milk Powder, Malted Milk Powder, and Other Dry Milk Products Shipped in Consumer Packages Weighing 3 Pounds or Less Excluding Nonfat Dry Milk and Infants' Formula in Japan, for £495 (Parker, 2006b). ICON's World Outlook series is data-driven, blending textual templates with automatically generated analytical tables visualising industry trends. For text-heavier content, ICON has published a Webster's series of reference books including the 116-page *Webster's Swedish to English Crossword Puzzles: Level 1* for £14.95 (Parker, 2007) and other crossword books to facilitate language learning, in addition to books comprising historical timelines and compilations of quotations, facts, and phrases. Most of these books are not just printed on demand – they are generated on demand.

In 2008, Parker's method of text production was brought to public attention through articles in news outlets like *The Guardian* (Abrahams, 2008) and *The New York Times* (Cohen, 2008). Articles about Parker's books have continued to be written since, each expressing the same sense of confusion as those initial 2008 articles: 'Meet the Robots Writing Your News Articles: The Rise of Automated Journalism', one is titled (McGuinness, 2014); 'Philip Parker's Trick For Authoring Over 1 Million Books: Don't Write', is another (Bosker, 2013); as is 'If an Algorithm Wrote This, How Would You Even Know?' (Podolny, 2015). Yet Parker himself, as quoted in one of these articles (Bosker, 2013), is hardly advocating the replacement of human authors by machines. 'There are very few implications for writers because we're covering areas that writers don't or can't cover,' he explains. 'All of these projects seem very diverse, but really they're all in same vein [*sic*]: we're using automation to reach areas that wouldn't have been served otherwise. And it gives people the opportunity to see or experience content they wouldn't have been able to otherwise.' According to Parker, his books are intended to supplement those that humans write, and to broaden the range of content available to readers with specialised needs and/or interests.

The review that opened this section was undoubtedly written in jest, poking fun at just *how* specialised *The 2007 Report on Facial Tissue Stock* is as a result of its automated processes of production. However, not all (potential) readers of these computer-generated books so readily find humour in the technology. One Amazon reviewer (Downey, 2015) for Parker's computer-generated *The Official Patient's Sourcebook on Acne Rosacea* (2002) warns:

> This book was written by a computer. Don't bother with it. See New York Times report March 8, 2015, 'If an Algorithm Wrote This, How Would You Even Know?' Philip M. Parker is the fraud who has a patented algorithmic system that has 'generated more than a million books, more than 100,000 of which are available on Amazon.' Buyer beware!! And Parker is NOT alone.

Another reviewer (Amazon Customer) of *Acne Rosacea* – posting 12 February 2004, prior to Parker's wave of publicity – advises potential buyers to instead take 'a trip to google.com, drop the "acne" bit at [*sic*] from "acne rosacea" and surf the first few sites you find. After that you will be in front of this book, and have something else to do with your $USD 25.' Such recommended surfing is, in actuality, akin to how Parker's system operates. Like a human researcher, the system sifts through a range of digital sources and consolidates information into a cohesive narrative. As indicated by the former comment, however, some readers do not think of NLG positively. 'This book was written by a computer' is, after all, more a fact than a judgement of textual quality. The former reviewer provides no explanation as to why a computer-generated text should be considered not worth reading, and depends on the review's readers reaching similar conclusions of their own accord. The other reviewer provides more detail, specifying why one should avoid buying this book: the text offers only a cursory overview of its subject. This reviewer (Amazon Customer, 2004) continues the criticism of *Acne Rosacea*, protesting that 'later they promise "a chapter dedicated to helping you find your peer groups". They end up only mentioning a prescription drug page at rosacea-control.com, CureZone and MedHelp (of which CureZone didn't mention rosacea at all, and MedHelp timed out). Again they never mention the NRS or the Rosacea Support Group.' The book, according to this reviewer, does not offer any unique insight into its subject, and is therefore unsatisfactory due to insufficient content rather than its production process. The former review emphasises production process over textual quality, exemplifying the symbolic value attributed to originality expected from human authorship. The inextricable relationship between content and form associates the printed word with the human-authored text, and Parker's decision to make his generated texts available in printed form evidently affronts the extant human-driven institutions that determine and distribute all that is fit for print. *Acne Rosacea*, alongside Parker's other generated books, challenges understandings of the printed word as a fundamentally human artefact, an expression of human intelligence, a product of an author with communicative intention.

3.2 The Emergence of the Author

The author has not always been regarded as an individual creative genius, as is now customary. For example, the material conditions of medieval manuscript production, as well as the widely held attitudes towards the function of the writer at that time, created circumstances of textual authority radically different from those of the modern age. The medieval writer was a systematic plagiarist of sorts, copying from a variety of source texts to compose his own (Goldschmidt, 1943: 88–93; 113). Medieval scholars showed little regard for the individual identities of their books' writers, focusing instead on the ancient truths the books held. The author was not an individual creative genius, but a messenger, a copyist with creative licence. Certainly, there were exceptions (Saenger, 1999: 137). On a societal scale, though, medieval writers produced content according to a markedly different set of readerly expectations for content originality.

Printing technology transformed the authorial landscape, and the work of E. Ph. Goldschmidt (1943), Elizabeth Eisenstein (1979), and Lucien Febvre and Henri-Jean Martin (1997) (to list only a few) all support the theory that print facilitated a shift away from anonymity and towards the 'cults of personality' (Eisenstein, 1979) that have come to characterise modern-day print culture. Of course, authorship did not develop wholly as a response to print; modern understandings of the author as an individual creative genius began to emerge as early as the shift from orality to literacy

(Havelock, 1980: 98). Further, cultural developments like the rise of liberalism and increasing privatisation also contributed to the movement away from anonymity and towards cults of personality, as well as these cults' resultant senses of textual authority. Eisenstein observes that 'the veritable explosion of "creative acts" during the seventeenth century – the so-called "century of genius" – can be explained partly by the great increase in possible permutations and combinations of ideas' made possible by cross-cultural interchanges and 'increased [textual] output directed at relatively stable markets': both factors promoted by the proliferation of print (Eisenstein, 1979: 75). In such views, print both influenced and was influenced by changing conceptions of individuality and authorship. Through its gradual crystallisation, print culture supported a shift in the cultural mindset wherein cults of personality that praised individual genius became commonplace. The technological developments related to print had social consequences: namely, the veneration of the author.

The growth of the printing trade contributed to more definitive demarcations of occupational roles. The publisher and printer, for example, became two people rather than one, each with defined duties. One of the most renowned models delineating printing occupations is Robert Darnton's Communications Circuit. Darnton (1982: 68) begins his Circuit with the Author and the Publisher, connected with a bidirectional arrow. The Circuit then moves consecutively to Printers (with a nod to Suppliers), then Shippers, Booksellers, and Readers (and Binders). The Circuit closes with a tentative unidirectional connection between Readers and Author. Contained within the Circuit are the pressures of the 'economic and social conjuncture', 'intellectual influences and publicity', and 'political and legal sanctions'. In this model, Darnton presents a rigid division of labour that emphasises a standard materiality of printed texts produced for profit. Such roles continue to broadly characterise today's book trade, upholding the symbolic value attributed to books by comprising numerous gatekeeper functions for all that is fit for print. Although Darnton designed his Communications Circuit for his own studies of eighteenth-century France, book historians have since applied it liberally to a range of analogue and digital contexts from the past and present day (e.g. Ray Murray and Squires, 2013; van der Weel, 2001).

One notable feature of Darnton's Circuit – perpetuated in subsequent applications – is its focus on the occupational agents (e.g. Suppliers, Booksellers, Binder) who execute the processes that constitute a text's lifespan, as opposed to the processes themselves. Therein lies an assumption of individual human agency throughout each component of the Circuit, expressed through occupation. Nevertheless, Darnton's emphasis actually appears to be on the technologies associated with print themselves, more than on the individuals engaging with those technologies. 'Printers' constitute a node in themselves; 'Suppliers' provide paper, ink, type, and labour; a 'Binder' ties the entire printed work together. While this Circuit initially appears centred on a social structure, most obviously through the explicit appreciation of an 'economic and social conjuncture' in the Circuit's centre, that social structure operates only in relation to the technologies it depends upon. The economic and social conjuncture is constrained by the technologies under consideration. Individuals represented by the Circuit's components are defined by their specialist professional roles, which stem from the divisions of labour that emerge from the increasing complexity of print's technological facets and industrialised processes.

Conventional modern understandings of authorship, as in Darnton's Circuit, are often of a skilled professional role operating within a greater network of specialist roles. For this discussion, it is significant that Darnton begins his Circuit with the singular author. The Circuit simply could not function without the author, as the author is portrayed as the initial – and independent – site of text production. All begins and – as per the tentative connection that Darnton (1982: 67) has still yet to expound save for a perfunctory 'Authors are readers themselves' – ends with the author. The aforementioned 'cults of personality' that have come to characterise print culture are manifest through this imagined author, the individual creative genius without whom print culture as we know it could not exist. Never mind that many instances of authorship are, in fact, collaborative efforts, and that both authorship and reading are continuous processes: social functions that inform and are informed by every aspect of an act of text-based communication. The author as represented in Darnton's Communications Circuit – and as commonly believed today – is the originator of a text.

3.3 Reader Responsibility and the Hermeneutic Contract

In the English-speaking world, a literate person's eyes are trained to decode the symbols of language (e.g. the alphabet, emoji) through linear motions (left to right and top to bottom). These linear motions were, to be sure, habitual in manuscript tradition. The printed book, though, 'intensified perspective and the fixed point of view,' as Marshall McLuhan (1994: 172) argues. Indeed, '[t]he new intensity of visual stress and private point of view in the first century of printing were united to the means of self-expression made possible by the typographic extension of man.' The printed word is thus not just an extension of the eye. Like the written word, it is also an extension of the mind of an individual, or a group of individuals, translating intangible thought into tangible form that overcomes constraints of time and space to communicate with anyone who shares the literacy required to read it; the printed word too extends the minds of those readers who engage in related interpretive acts. The proliferation of print has arguably contributed to a restructuring of human thought processes, as typographical '[u]niformity, predictability, consistency, and standardisation were prerequisites for [the] analytical and scientific thinking' that defines modern rationality (van der Weel, 2011a: 85). The ingrained notion of printed texts as expository and linear, requiring mental concentration and patience, seeps into the human psyche more generally, contributing to what Adriaan van der Weel has dubbed the Order of the Book.

As van der Weel (2011a: 91) observes, our modern conception of democracy, mainly representative democracy, rests on the assumptions that all participating individuals (1) can access informative texts and (2) can read those texts. The Order of the Book assigns high symbolic value to books (especially in codex form), and to the printed word specifically, because the texts contained within these books direct the operation of social institutions (e.g. governmental policies) and contribute to the formation of shared social consciousness. Although much social interaction currently occurs in digital forms, these forms are commonly regarded as ephemeral, and important digital texts are often printed out for future reference or safekeeping. Printed texts also perpetuate cultural and literary heritage through a 'pastness of the past' (Goody and Watt, 1963: 311) established by an imagined antiquity that reflects contemporary ideologies informed by social understandings of self in relation to the past, the present, and predictions for the future (Anderson, 2006: 44–5). That one has invested the time to write a text, and that further people have invested the time and money to edit, print, distribute, and read that text contributes to the printed word's perceived significance. The printed word is always a social artefact with communicative value. However, it is an artefact disembodied from its creator through the mechanised and communal processes of its production.

While the printed word may appear neutral, disconnected from its writer, any communicative act necessitates a message, a message sender, and a message recipient. For printed texts the sender is generally considered the author; the recipient, the reader. The reader anticipates the text as a product of communicative intention, a conscious effort to convey a predetermined message, an embodiment of human agency informed by lived experience. The reader must interpret the message, whether through conscious consideration or wilful disregard of authorial intention. Either way, the reader embodies the text through an imagined author, and establishes a perceived contract with that author. I call this author–reader relationship 'the hermeneutic contract'. The hermeneutic contract is rooted in an underlying assumption that through language we articulate and legitimise lived experiences to ourselves and others. This is not to argue for linguistic determinism, wherein a language constrains its users' thought processes, but for a softer stance of linguistic relativity, wherein a language affects its users' cognition. Our perceptions of the world, and others' perceptions of ourselves, are shaped – but not necessarily wholly constrained – by the words at our disposal. It is through language that interpersonal agency is exercised, and that potentialities are realised.

Computer-generated texts in their current state, however, bring the hermeneutic contract into question. The hermeneutic contract's communication principle rests on the assumption that readers believe that authors want their texts to be both interesting and understandable. However, the author of a computer-generated text is an uncertain figure: human, computer, some combination thereof, or non-existent. Yet our current Order of the Book depends upon literacy as a means for full social participation; this dependency is based on an understanding of texts as being of social –

interpersonal, *human* – value. Where, then, does algorithmic authorship fit within the Order of the Book, a print-based culture with largely standardised textual artefacts? How are we to negotiate this new relationship between form and content, to appraise the status and value of texts to which our conventional hermeneutic contract may no longer apply?

3.4 Textual Interpretation and Ownership

D. F. McKenzie's notion of the 'sociology of texts' accentuates the communicative underpinnings of media and textual artefacts. The sociology of texts emphasises texts as being produced, transmitted, and received within unique sociocultural circumstances that inform their interpretation and use. It holds that 'the claim then is no longer for their [texts'] truth as one might seek to define that by an authorial intention, but their testimony as defined by their historical use' (McKenzie, 1999: 29). A sociology of texts, in essence, recognises textual artefacts as extensions of human agency that is manifest in various forms throughout production, transmission, and reception. A textual artefact may have myriad potential meanings, all emerging from personalised interactions with that artefact occurring within particular sociocultural contexts.

The sociology of texts is complemented by other social theories of media like the Social Construction of Technology (SCOT) framework. The SCOT framework hinges upon the 'interpretive flexibility' that encompasses each social group's unique hermeneutic responses to an artefact, which are informed by the group's own perceived needs and contextual circumstances (Pinch and Bijker, 1984: 410–29). Stanley Fish's (1980: 167–73) notion of 'interpretive communities' is an equivalent argument in literary studies, which Simone Murray (2018b) has revisited for her investigation into online reading communities from a book history perspective. Distinguishing all the potential meanings bred from a text is hardly possible, but appreciation of that which exists outside the artefact itself shifts attention from being fixed solely on the text towards more comprehensive understandings of that text's diverse past and present applications. The very concept of authorship is similarly murky, existing within particular social situations and within complex social and economic networks; such circumstances are largely defined by contemporary literate mentalities and dominant media for text production and dissemination. The author is a culturally constructed figure, specific both within her individuality and position in time and space. A writer may be a corporal individual, but an author represents the social circumstances to which that corporal writer has grown accustomed. By applying a sociology of texts' outward gaze, we may situate today's computer-generated texts within the greater sociocultural contexts in which they exist: namely, those contexts related to conceptions of authorship and the assumed relationships between authors and readers.

In print's infancy, the first printer to publish a text tended to hold the exclusive privileges to copy and reprint that text in perpetuity, with authors receiving lump sums for their manuscripts upfront. In England, this entitlement was granted by the Stationers' Company, a guild formed in 1403 that protected the economic interests of card-carrying members of the book trade involved in text production and dissemination. Members of the Company were granted ownership of published texts by entering those texts in the Company Register, which served as an antecedent to modern copyright registration. When Queen Mary I granted the Stationers' Company its Royal Charter in 1557, the Company was legally empowered to censor texts that offended the religious, political, or social regimes of the day. The Stationers' Company thereby restricted the production of a text to one printer, and ensured that texts adhered to a social standard that did not explicitly challenge the values and ideologies of the ruling elite.

Changing cultural values, however, led to diminished power for the Stationers' Company. The year 1710 saw the passing of the Statute of Anne, commonly regarded as the world's first copyright statute (for nuance, see Schoff Curtin, 2017). The Statute's extended name offers insight into its purposes: 'An Act for the Encouragement of Learning, by Vesting the Copies of Printed Books in the Authors or Purchasers of such Copies, during the Times therein mentioned.' The Statute of Anne declared that copyright in perpetuity, as was the Stationers' Company's custom, made knowledge too expensive and exclusive, as a lack of competition allowed a text's copyright holder to set its price at an inaccessible amount. The Statute made it so that copyrights were only valid for either fourteen or twenty-one years (whether the text was published after or before the

Statute's enactment, respectively), and then had to be renewed or otherwise fall into the public domain, mimicking the contemporary legal treatment of patents. What is more, the Statute was the first act to recognise the legal rights of authors, with the author – rather than the printer – being granted control over the copying of their text. Where authorship and ownership were once distinct, they were now coincident.

Despite the Statute of Anne's proclaimed objective for the 'Encouragement of Learning', financial gain has always been a motivation driving copyright, and altruism does not make money. Thus, while the Statute of Anne was legally enacted, works remained copyrighted in perpetuity for the printers under common law, despite some high-profile judicial cases involving individuals citing the Statute for protection after they had printed texts whose copyrights had expired (Deazley, 2008). When the Statute was finally upheld in the 1774 landmark *Donaldson v Becket* case, printers finally had legal affirmation of their choices to produce inexpensive reprints of popular texts that the Statute deemed to be within the public domain. Literacy rates began to rise at an unprecedented rate, heightening demand for printed texts and subsequently increasing both the number of titles available and the size of print runs. There were, to be sure, other reasons for rising literacy rates: public education initiatives, increased access to circulating libraries, the establishment of coffee house culture, and heightened dependency upon textual means for distribution of civic notices, to list just a few (Cowan, 2012; Houston, 1993: 374–80). The demand for texts was both initiated and fulfilled by the production capacity of contemporary printing technology; the increased presence of texts heightened the demand for more. From the interplay of technological development and socioeconomic circumstances, mass readerships gradually emerged to consume the texts of individual authors who were granted cultural authority by virtue of their occupation. The modern conception of the author as an individual in an occupational role was formalised, leading to a new means for personal financial gain: literary celebrity.

The proliferation of digital media has nuanced the conventional understanding of the author as literary celebrity and cultural authority. Matthew Kirschenbaum, for one, considers the traditional author role not as disappearing, but as being supplemented by an '@uthor' role. Writing in the

Los Angeles Review of Books, Kirschenbaum (2015) observes 'a landscape of authorship and reading that is no longer confined to simple geometries and lines of influence, and no longer served by the established critical schools.' According to Kirschenbaum, the @uthor exists within increasingly digital contexts that enable new forms of author–reader interaction; his article draws most of its examples from Twitter. In Kirschenbaum's view, such new digital availabilities – principally social media platforms – allow for the public performance of authorial identities in ways that appear more spontaneous than staged. In her recent book about 'reading, writing, and selling books in the Internet era', Simone Murray (2018a: 22–52) makes a similar argument, framing authorship in today's digital ecology and economy as a conscious ongoing performance. Likewise, Gillian Beer (2014: 1) writes about the modern interplay between author and reader. Referring specifically to digital means of distribution, Beer argues that '[t]he link between human person and made work has gathered intensity exactly in the face of new technology that more and more disperses authority: not only copyright but the intactness of text as a good are now in question. But readers flock to hear, see, and meet the author.'

Kirschenbaum, Murray, and Beer all recognise modern readers' apparent inability to separate the work from its creator. The work and creator are conceptually bound, as we search for the author embedded within the text to contextualise its production. Digital developments like social media platforms facilitate connections between authors and readers and, while readers are most certainly able to interpret texts as they deem appropriate, curiosity about a work's creator can now be so quickly satisfied that authorial embodiment has been reasserted as an almost inevitable part of modern interpretive processes. This is not to say that the author's interpretation of a text is final. Using William Faulkner's 1957–1958 University of Virginia classroom conferences to illustrate the flexibility of interpretation, Kirschenbaum (2015) writes that 'no one accepts Faulkner's utterances as the ultimate authority on his work. We're too sophisticated for that, and Faulkner himself cautioned that his statements and self-representations were that of a "man in motion." That is, Faulkner the person understood himself to be in dialogue with his own public image.' Readers flocked to hear, see, and meet Faulkner. Yet his authority over his own work was already dispersed in 1958, and is ever more dispersed as the implications of the digital, notably ready access to various textual interpretations, are pronounced. Indeed, the corporal Faulkner is not an author. Rather, readers' imagined versions of Faulkner – rooted in their interpretations of Faulkner's texts and public persona, as well as other critics' interpretations of his work – constitute his authorship, and it is this imagined author with whom readers engage in their textual relationships.

In any act of reading there is a balance struck between author and reader: the hermeneutic contract. This balance exists regardless of genre, although conventions associated with a text's genre may induce slightly different reading approaches and understandings of authorial intention. 'The reader resists; the reader complies; the reader identifies; the reader re-makes the text, not only in the light of the evidence provided but also in the presence of an unuttered speaking voice, now speaking inside us,' Gillian Beer (2014: 5–6) writes. 'The author as adversary equals the reader as adversary: the two entwine and collaborate, *within the reader*.' For Beer, it is the reader who negotiates the author–reader balance. The reader controls the reading experience, and the primary responsibility for textual interpretation and the decoding of any communicated messages lies with the messages' receiver rather than with the messages' transmitter. Other scholars have similarly observed reader-centrism facilitated by the searching, personalisation, and participatory opportunities afforded by digital technologies like the Web (van der Weel, 2014: 42–3). Computer-generated texts in particular stress the responsibility of the reader as meaning-maker. After all, there are no readings, signings, appearances, or interviews for the NLG system. Further, the link between person and made work is often uncertain, with an ambiguous balance between computational contributions and human intervention. While algorithmic authorship may represent – to repurpose Beer's words – a 'new technology that more and more disperses authority', readers nevertheless continue seeking to embody the familiar figure of the author, tethered to the understanding of a text as a means for interpersonal communication. In his 1995 'manifesto for computer literature', Jean-Pierre Balpe (30 [translation my own]) considers the implications of computer-generated texts for conventional understandings of authorship. For computer-generated texts 'more than anywhere else,' he argues, 'the author would be a fiction of the texts. This will be our final point, but it will remain unresolved.' In Balpe's view, the computer-generated text 'destabilises' the reader because its words 'are emitted by an inaccessible, superiorly reassuring mind' rather than by an embodied author with whom one could in principle debate a text's meaning (Balpe, 1995: 29). The computer-generated text stimulates readers to consider their acts of reading and meaning-making, to acknowledge and adapt their own senses of reader responsibility. The reader's relationship with the author – the hermeneutic contract – is at the forefront of such consideration.

3.5 *Institutions of Knowledge Dissemination and Production*

Texts are artefacts separated from their creators through institutionalised processes of production and dissemination, with the primary responsibility for reconnecting artefacts and creators resting with readers. Readerly re-embodiment of the author is the subject of Jorge Luis Borges' short story 'Pierre Menard, Author of the *Quixote*' (1999), which praises the fictional Menard for his authorial genius in copying verbatim two chapters of Miguel de Cervantes' *Don Quixote*. As Borges' story highlights, the perceived identity of the author is important because answers to questions of authorship attribution reflect conceptions of both financial and cultural capital. Authorship supports the articulation of an individual's voice, ownership supports capitalism's commodification of the individual, and together authorship and ownership (under the title of authorship) represent a creative economy rooted in an expectation of communicative intention compelled by individual agency. However, digital media have confronted the more general convention of authorship as constituting a distinct occupational role. For example, a popular desktop publishing software like Microsoft Word fundamentally alters one's writing process through its graphical user interface that allows for quick and easy structural changes. The software may even suggest alternative spellings or grammar usage, eliciting questions about whether a writer's use of desktop publishing software may be seen as a kind of co-authorship with the computer. In a similar vein, Web-based self-publishing platforms like Amazon's Kindle Direct Publishing and Lulu reduce the traditional publisher role to a series of text boxes for the

author to complete (see Skains, 2019 for more examples). Indeed, occupational roles associated with print become blurred and altogether indistinguishable in the consideration of a system that cannot easily develop
a distinct institutional order. Philip Parker's patented algorithms are
combined to generate, market, and distribute books, but one cannot
readily ascertain precisely which part of Parker's system does what, or
how involved Parker himself has been in the production of any one book.
In an increasingly digital world, the author continues to assert cultural
authority, but the kind of cultural authority asserted has changed.
Through digital media that permit online exchange, the author appears
more embodied than ever before, a personal figure who can respond
directly to readers through social media platforms and who may exist
outside of her own texts or even the literary realm altogether (e.g. as
a political figure or an actor). At the same time, the author – masked by
the character she performs in an appeal to literary celebrity, or perhaps
replaced by a patented set of algorithms – remains a largely imagined
figure, further disembodied from texts she has produced not only by the
medium of print, but by the additional production and dissemination
processes induced by digital development.

But it is the writer who determines the content of a text and, even in
instances of interactive or hypertextual prose, how that content is presented.
Adriaan van der Weel (2011a: 178–9) refers to this authority as the 'interpretive burden', and argues that the interpretive burden is ever shifting
'from the instigator of the communication to its recipient' in increasingly
digital circumstances. 'More generally, the emphasis in digital communications is shifting increasingly from the transfer of knowledge (where readers
can in principle remain passive, trusting their source) to the transfer of
information which can lead to knowledge,' he writes. 'The reader bears
a heavier responsibility for at least the validation of knowledge, but more
often also for its constitution.' It is important for this discussion to distinguish between information and knowledge. Information refers to data that
have been systematically structured or presented in a way that connects
meaningful data points. A list of facts, for example, provides information.
Knowledge, however, refers to the critical analysis of information and the
understanding of how to apply that information meaningfully to social

situations (Ackoff, 1989: 3–9). To one who is about to venture outdoors, a statement like 'the sky is grey and cloudy' is information; that person's knowledge is reflected when she chooses to wear waterproof boots and bring an umbrella. When van der Weel writes about the transfer of knowledge, he is referring to the textual sharing of perceptions informed by personal lived experiences, which may in turn be perceived by readers altogether differently from the ways expected. Knowledge entails not only recognition of patterns and trends within information, but also awareness of what those patterns and trends mean within their surrounding sociocultural circumstances. However, each reader exists within unique circumstances. It is therefore not appropriate to adopt the formalist view of reading wherein a reader simply follows the text, consuming content at face value. The reader considers a text's content in light of her own understanding of the world, opting to in some way accept the writer's knowledge into her own worldview, or disregard it completely.

Many current applications of algorithmic authorship appear to tend towards conveying information rather than knowledge. One such example is Valtteri the Election Bot (Valtteri, n.d.), an NLG system developed by a Finnish research team called Immersive Automation (see Immersive Automation, n.d.) between December 2016 and May 2018, financially backed by numerous public and private Finnish organisations. Valtteri populated generic human-written English, Finnish, and Swedish templates with public election results retrieved from the Finnish Ministry of Justice. This is a similar production process to that of Urbs Media, described in the Introduction, wherein humans write text-based templates with blanks for the NLG system to populate with relevant variables for highly localised content generation. What distinguished Valtteri's functionality was its user-centricity. Through Valtteri's Web interface, users could determine which electoral district, municipality, polling station, party, or candidate they wanted the system to generate an article about. One article, entitled 'The Finns Party drop most seats across Finland', begins with the following paragraph:

> The Finns Party dropped the most council seats throughout Finland and lost 425 seats. The party got 3.5 percentage points fewer votes than in the last municipal election and

decreased their voter support by the greatest margin. The
party dropped 80501 votes since the last municipal election
and has 770 seats in the new council.

Each succeeding paragraph focuses on a different political party involved in
the April 2017 Finnish municipal elections, providing the same kind of
information in a slightly varied order. While the text's sentences adhere to
rules of English syntax, the piece has limited linguistic flourish or variation.
Further, while the article does compare party performances to previous
elections, it offers no explicit data analysis that could aid the reader in
situating election results within historical or current societal trends. The
reader is tasked with forming knowledge from information to justify the
relevance of data to current cultural conversations. The interpretive embel-
lishments that one may expect from a human-written text are omitted, and
readers without awareness of Finnish politics are thoroughly disadvan-
taged. This is an article for those with a high level of assumed knowledge
about Finnish politics.

According to its developers, Valtteri was intended to serve human
journalists by identifying potentially newsworthy information, rather than
replace the human author altogether. In one case study analysis, the
developers (Leppänen et al., 2017: 181) note that '[t]he automation of
finding news in the era of increased availability of data sources ensures
that media companies efficiently make use of the data and report even on
the "small fish" news which they would not have had the time or
resources to report.' For practical applications, '[t]his means that they
are able to cover news that is of interest to even local or small audiences,
thus improving business offering[s] and providing added value to audiences.' For Valtteri's developers, one of the main benefits imparted by an
automated news generation system is the system's ability to overcome the
traditional practice of gatekeeping, whereby text producers determine
what content readers should be shown. With a system like Valtteri, the
reader may freely commission articles that reflect her own personal
interests. As Valtteri's developers (Leppänen et al., 2017: 182) claim,
'[t]he system can produce as many news articles as possible and put the
power of selection in the reader's hands.' Gatekeeping, however, is an

integral feature of the Order of the Book. The investment of numerous individuals' time and money in a text's production contributes to the value attributed to that text. The academic practice of peer review is only one example of how such gatekeeping establishes a source as reputable and trustworthy. Yet systems like Valtteri undermine those human-controlled systems that exist to dictate selection and publication. Instead, it is the reader who determines that which is fit to print. Subsequently, it is the reader who determines what information means in more general contexts. The reader, rather than the author, converts information into knowledge. The interpretive burden shifts increasingly to the reader, as the gatekeeper role appears diminished.

3.6 Hyper-Individualism

This elevated role of the reader affirms a greater societal shift towards what I identify here as 'hyper-individualism'. Hyper(-)individualism as a term has already been used intermittently in discussions of psychology, media, and culture (Gauchet, 2000; Lake, 2017). The term as it is used here, though, is unconnected with these previous uses, given a lack of consistent definition. In this discussion, hyper-individualism is characterised by each person's tendency towards self-gratification, which itself is driven by senses of self-importance and uniqueness that together manifest in a sense of entitlement to highly personalised content conforming to individual worldviews. This sense of entitlement is supported by algorithmic filters in, for example, online search engines or social media feeds that offer customised results based on an individual's Web history. Individualism refers to consumers seeking personalisation through their own curation of media. Hyper-individualism more strongly acknowledges the pervasiveness of personalisation in both analogue and digital forms. Media are curated by individuals, as well as by algorithmic filters, both conspicuous and concealed. Contrary to the uniformity and standardisation promoted by print, algorithmic authorship promotes mass personalisation by generating texts for readerships of one.

The greater cultural discourse is shifting away from privileging the author as an authority over a text, and fragmentedly towards each individual reader. Indeed, digital technologies, of which NLG is only one, allow for increased involvement of readers in processes of text production, fundamentally changing the conventional relationship between author and reader. In many instances, the author is no longer so much one who transfers knowledge, but a co-creator with the reader. In both printed and digital texts, the reader largely remains at the mercy of the writer's direction, given the finite number of paths the reader may select from to journey through the text. Nevertheless, digital texts like those produced using Valtteri's interactive Web interface may afford the reader a new relationship with the text: one in which the reader assembles it, rather than watching it unfurl. Although the number of paths the reader may choose from might be limited, the reader's involvement in a text's unfurling contributes to a sense of control over the text as one navigates through it, affirming the reader's senses of individual agency and importance. Of course, the argument that reading is never linear – that readers' eyes skip between lines of text, that readers may not read one text from beginning to end without pause, and so forth – has so long been commonplace that it may now be considered trite. Few readings can ever be strictly linear, given humans' predisposition to distraction. Moreover, Web-based hypertext normalises non-linear reading practices, as the reader must navigate through not just one text, but many. These texts are written collaboratively, are presented in different visual formats, may be supplemented with other media such as video or sound clips, or may radically deviate the reader to a new subject via hyperlink. In such modern digital contexts, it is the reader who is tasked with making sense of this proliferation of texts, and information more generally.

Recall the distinction between information and knowledge. Information refers to data that have been systematically structured or presented in a way that connects meaningful points. Knowledge refers to the critical analysis of information and the understanding of how to use that information meaningfully. In the conventional hermeneutic contract, the author is understood to be transferring knowledge to the reader. If a text is regarded as an extension of an individual, it follows that what is written will reflect the subjective experiences of the individual writing. Even in instances of the avant-garde, seemingly unintelligible texts are seen as the result of communicative intention that the reader is left to decipher. It is the author who encodes a text with meaning, and the reader who decodes that text. Yet in a hypertext-heavy world wherein the reader faces a bombardment of texts seemingly less linear and stable than conventional human-written texts, the reader must make sense of where each of these texts fits within more general contexts (van der Weel, 2011b: 46). The critical analysis of information and the understanding of how to use that information meaningfully is undertaken by the reader, affirming a societal shift towards hyper-individualism that is supported by inflated senses of self, resulting from a prioritisation of individualistic self-expression. With ever-increasing access to vast amounts of information in various analogue and digital forms, individual readers are not only welcome to interpret textual material according to their personal worldviews, but encouraged to generate knowledge themselves.

Yet individualised generation of knowledge rather than mere access to formal knowledge contained in books has very real implications for conceptions of citizenship and full participation in representative democracy. Writing from the perspective of a sociologist of technology, Mike Michael (2014: 52–3) draws attention to a shift wherein '[r]ather than educating the public so that they can take up their roles as scientific citizens, they are to be consulted.' As a result, '[c]itizenship here is no longer about having sufficient knowledge, or being asked to deliberate over a range of preset technological options; it is about having a say in the development of research programs, in agenda setting in research funding, in prioritization of sociopolitical goals.' Rather than having one cultural authority to consult – an author, with printed formal knowledge – we now have countless cultural authorities comprising a heterogeneous 'public', many of whom are wary of the hierarchies of institutions related to communications and media. While this is by no means a new phenomenon (see, for example, Gregory and Miller, 1998), the tendency towards populist anti-intellectualism in modern rhetoric has been associated with recent political happenings like the 2016 referendum for the United Kingdom's withdrawal from the European Union, as well as the result of the United States' 2016 presidential election (Motta, 2018). Evidently stemming from an underlying scepticism of expert knowledge and institutionalised hierarchy, anti-intellectualism is the product of a hyper-individualised culture that has so deeply internalised the values of individualistic facets of representative democracy that the individual expects not only external validation for personal thoughts, but also means for voicing and affirming subjective experiences and worldviews.

The individualistic desire for affirmation may partially explain why companies specialising in the computer generation of data-driven news articles and business reports have seen commercial success. Arria NLG, Automated Insights, Narrative Science, and Phrasee are only a few of these companies; they have all partnered with high-profile organisations like the Associated Press and Microsoft to rapidly generate content for mass and niche readerships alike. For a computer-generated business report, an NLG system draws from quantified measures of productivity, processing these measures to present data-driven assertions of each individual's strengths and weaknesses relative to other employees. Similarly, the functionality of these systems may be applied to smaller-scale events not otherwise covered by public news outlets. Narrative Science, for one, has partnered with GameChanger – a baseball, softball, and basketball scorekeeping application – 'to craft newspaper quality "Game Recap Stories." Within minutes of the final out, a recap is instantly generated, and available online and in the app' (Anon., 2016b). GameChanger's services are primarily marketed towards followers of minor-league teams, including youth teams generally excluded from media coverage due to lack of widespread interest. Narrative Science and GameChanger's collaboration lets parents read stories about their children's games – to see their children's names in 'newspaper quality' articles – rather than require them to sift through less appealing numeric databases. As any parent familiar with Little League sports reports will know, though, there is an art to writing these texts. Players are always portrayed positively, and games resulting in losses are always framed as valiant battles rather than miserable struggles. The GameChanger game recaps adhere to the expected format and language usage of the genre. With this technology, any Little League game can be transmuted into a cohesive narrative contributing to a sense of professionalism in the league, as well as lasting excitement amongst fans. One recap, for example, reviews a local baseball game played by ten- and eleven-year-olds. Despite the Oakville team losing to Vaughan, 'Evan T triggered Oakville A's 11 U AAA's comeback,' and '[a]fter pushing across two runs in the bottom of the fifth, Oakville A's 11 U AAA faced just a 5–3 deficit' (Anon., 2016a).

Each of the generated GameChanger articles concludes with a disclaimer that the article has been 'Powered by Narrative Science and GameChanger

Media', but no description of the text's production process accompanies the article itself. The text seems to be a typical baseball report, with readers uninformed of its generated nature unless they actively seek additional information about Narrative Science. On a larger scale, Narrative Science has also collaborated with the Big Ten Network to provide recaps of college sporting events throughout the United States. These generated articles used to be accompanied by an editor's note at their conclusion, indicating that '[i]n partnership with Narrative Science, BTN.com posts fast recaps after every half of every Big Ten men's basketball game. Use the links above for more info on this specific game' (BTN.com Staff, 2013). Earlier, the articles had been accompanied by an even briefer note of their being 'Powered by Narrative Science', with a link to Narrative Science's website (BTN.com Staff, 2012). More recent generated articles include no disclaimer related to text production.

Such disclaimers are so equivocal as to be almost meaningless, though, and the reader must actively seek additional information about Narrative Science to learn that an article has been computer-generated. In these instances, it appears that it is not only readers who are aware of the symbolic value attributed to human authorship, but also the companies who specialise in wide-ranging applications of algorithmic authorship. In one study of numerous international organisations that use news content generators, researchers (Montal and Reich, 2017) observed what they called a 'transparency gap': organisations avoiding full disclosure regarding the origins of their computer-generated stories. Tiptoeing around issues of authorship, organisations may share clues about NLG having factored into article production, but omit any mention of algorithmic authorship that may spur negative reactions similar to those expressed by the reviewers of Parker's *Acne Rosacea*. Despite the success of other NLG systems' personalised outputs, companies reaping rewards from the mass production of computer-generated articles appear attuned to the potential for reader resistance, and therefore withhold production details.

3.7 Conclusion

Algorithmic authorship affronts the conventional author–reader relationship – the hermeneutic contract – through hyper-individualistic personalisation of reading experiences. Such personalisation may take the form of individualised interpretations of texts, or of the computational production of texts for singular readerships. Using historical and modern references, this section has shown that 'author' is hardly a static term, and that technological and social developments have led to markedly different judgements of textual authority. Likewise, the role of the reader has changed over time. NLG, like other technologies associated with text production, prompts reconsideration of textual functions and processes of interpretation.

Where, then, does the conventional hermeneutic contract belong in considerations of computer-generated texts? The establishment of the hermeneutic contract rests almost entirely with the reader, who acknowledges a relationship – however imaginary – with an author. As with human-written texts, readers assume that computer-generated texts are produced with some sort of communicative intention, to be both interesting and understandable to an intended readership. The assumption of communicative intention is reinforced when human writers appear increasingly embodied through use of social media platforms and other digital media. At the same time, the fragmentary nature of modern digital culture enables readers to become increasingly responsible for crafting knowledge from vast amounts of information, becoming what Mike Michael (2014: 52–3) calls 'scientific citizens', who are to be encouraged to participate in policy decisions and agenda setting. NLG amplifies such social fragmentation, as texts may not just be interpreted by individual readers, but actually produced for them. In such cases, the hermeneutic contract seems to maintain its relevance because the responsibility for maintaining such a contract has little to do with who (or what) the author actually is, and more to do with the reader's perceptions of the author. As with a human-written text, the author of a computer-generated text is largely imagined by the reader. The next section ponders the language that should be used to describe the algorithmic author.

4 Algorithmic Authorship and Agency

4.1 Introduction

The date is 1st November 2017. The place is Amersfoort, the Netherlands. Inside de Bibliotheek Eemland (the Eemland Library), an excited group has gathered for the launch of the annual Nederland Leest (Netherlands Reads) campaign. Run by De Stichting Collectieve Propaganda van het Nederlandse Boek (the Foundation for the Collective Promotion for the Dutch Book), an organisation that promotes Dutch literacy and literature, Nederland Leest distributes free copies of a selected text in libraries across the country each November, sparking discussion about the year's selected theme. In 2017, this theme was robotics. The selected text was Isaac Asimov's *Ik, robot* (*I, Robot*), a collection of short stories about human–robot interaction. Nederland Leest's reissued edition of *Ik, robot*, though, concluded with a new story: 'De robot van de machine is de mens' (literally, 'The Robot of the Machine is Human'). This story was written by popular Dutch author Ronald Giphart – and co-authored by an NLG system called the Asibot (Karsdorp et al., 2017).

Throughout the room two-foot-tall Nao robots (developed by SoftBank Robotics) are scattered, with event attendees eagerly instructing them to stand up and sit down, and engaging them in small talk. On the stage stands four-foot-tall Pepper, a sleek humanoid robot (also developed by SoftBank Robotics). Upon walking onto the stage to begin the event, master of ceremonies Diana Matroos briefly converses with Pepper as though she were meeting a person. Throughout the programme, the Nao robots and Pepper are used to testify to advancements in robotics, and Pepper occasionally pipes up to contribute to the hour-long discussion about the social value of robotics and mechanisation. Audience members are asked whether they agree or disagree with a series of statements related to the future of robotics: for example, 'robots can make good art: agree or disagree?' Voting with their Nederland Leest paddles – with a robot's head on one side and Giphart's face on the other – the audience's opinion is split fairly evenly. Then, the moment finally comes to officially launch the new edition of

Ik, robot. On the stage stands Ronald Giphart, positioned next to Arie Rommers, user of one of the world's most advanced prosthetic hands. Rommers stands between Giphart and a large robot arm, which has been placed on a platform adorned with a ceremonious red tablecloth. Kraftwerk's 1978 'The Robots' blasts through the sound system. Slowly, the robot arm lifts a copy of the new edition of *Ik, robot*, turning to pass it to Rommers. From robot to cyborg, and then from cyborg to human, Rommers passes the book to Giphart, who triumphantly raises it towards the audience. The room erupts in applause.

At the event's reception, attendees excitedly collect their free copies of *Ik, robot*, flipping swiftly to the final chapter by Giphart and the Asibot. Representatives for the Nao robots and Pepper stand with their machines, answering questions about the technologies they are touting. The Nao robots are used in community centres like libraries and seniors' homes to dispel fears of new technology; Pepper is used as a novelty in service-based businesses and corporate events. All representatives assure attendees that these robots repond to users through series of programmed responses. 'It's just a puppet,' one representative asserts. 'He just does what you tell him to do.'[2]

4.2 NLG Systems as Tools

Computers have long been employed as tools for creating textual artefacts. In a practical sense, users engage with the technology according to its capacities. Word-processing software, for example, offers immediate feedback on potential spelling and grammar errors, while a typewriter does not. The human and the human's writing tools co-evolve and co-exist, with this symbiosis influencing processes of text production, dissemination, and reception. For aesthetic purposes, human–computer symbiosis has led to text production through such initiatives as the ALAMO (Atelier de Littérature Assistée par la Mathématique et les Ordinateurs – literature workshop assisted by mathematics and computers) (ALAMO, n.d.), an ongoing effort proposed by Oulipians Paul Braffort and Jacques Roubaud in 1981 to promote

---

[2] Anonymised Pepper representative, conversation with the author
(1 November 2017, Amersfoort).

experimentation with literature through computerised systematisation and controlled randomisation. In such cases, Margaret Boden (2010: 184–5) argues that it is the computer artist (i.e. developer) who is responsible for what input a system will respond to, how the system will respond, how unpredictable the system's output will be, and how transparent the system's functionality will be to users. Even the most unpredictable output, for Boden, results from choices the computer artist has made. Likewise, Jay David Bolter (1991: 187) has remarked that '[t]he autonomy of the computer is only apparent. The computer seems to be a tool that one can let go of, but all programs, including AI programs, simply defer the need to return to the human user.' Elsewhere, Bolter (1984: 232–3) explains that '[t]he computer is in some ways a grand machine in the Western mechanical-dynamic tradition and in other ways a tool-in-hand from the ancient craft tradition. The best way to encourage the humane use of computers is to emphasize, where possible, the second heritage over the first, the tool over the machine.' Although a developer may not be able to predict a system's exact output, the output reflects choices the developer has made while programming, as well as choices the user has made while engaging with the system.

One recent work that exemplifies the NLG system as tool is Zach Whalen's *The Several Houses of Brian, Spencer, Liam, Victoria, Brayden, Vincent, and Alex*, a product of the 2017 National Novel Generation Month (NaNoGenMo). Initiated in 2013 by Darius Kazemi (see Kazemi, n.d.), NaNoGenMo is a spin-off of the popular National Novel Writing Month (NaNoWriMo), when participants are challenged to write a novel of 50,000 words or more each November. In NaNoGenMo, though, participants do not write their novels themselves. Instead, they must write codes capable of generating 50,000-word novels. While NaNoWriMo defines a novel as an extended piece of fiction, Kazemi explains (see nanogenmo.github.io) that in NaNoGenMo '[t]he "novel" is defined however you want. It could be 50,000 repetitions of the word "meow". It could literally grab a random novel from Project Gutenberg. It doesn't matter, as long as it's 50k+ words.' Since its inception, NaNoGenMo participants have submitted hundreds of computer-generated novels reflecting a wide range of subjects and generation methods. In 2014, one participant (hugovk, 2014) generated *50,000 Meows*, which changed all of the words in classic works such as

Melville's *Moby Dick* into meows of the same length; 'Better sleep with a sober cannibal than a drunken Christian' translated to 'Meeoow meoow meow m meeow meooooow meow m meeeeow Meoooooow.' In 2015, another participant (Regan) wrote a code that identified the nearest named colour for every pixel of a digital photograph of a cover image for Hemingway's *The Sun Also Rises*; the novel, totalling more than 803,000 words, comprises a list of these colours beginning with 'Quartz. Davy's grey. Purple taupe. Gray.' These kinds of works exemplify the unique potentialities of NLG as a means for text production. Whalen's *Several Houses* takes a more traditional form, mimicking a typical children's book, including large, colourful text and striking imagery. Each 'house' is a story that adopts the form of the classic nursery rhyme 'This Is the House That Jack Built'. Page spreads are split into two parts: illustrations on the left, text on the right. 'This is the SLEEP that eluded the WORRIED PERSON that lay in the BED that rested the PERSON that armed the WEAPON that hurt the PERSON that headed for the HOUSE that Spencer built,' reads page 128, which is accompanied by an image of a house blurred by pastel watercolours and overlaid with images like a person, a gun, and a bed (Whalen, 2018b).

To generate *Several Houses*, Whalen wrote a program that builds chains of textual concepts ending in 'house'. These chains are developed by referencing ConceptNet, a free online semantic network that links meanings of words to teach computers the nuances of language and intricacies of human knowledge using machine learning methods. The accompanying illustrations likewise stemmed from Whalen's code. Another program selects a relevant icon from the Noun Project's free online repository of icons, colours that icon, and then randomly places it on the page on top of another Creative Commons image of a house, which itself has been randomly selected from Flickr and coloured using a 'watercolor' function on free image-editing software ImageMagick (Whalen, 2018a). As per NaNoGenMo's rules, Whalen has publicly shared the source codes for both the text and the illustrations; more tech-savvy readers may generate novels in this style for themselves (Whalen, 2018b and 2019).

Whalen's *Several Houses* demonstrates the human–computer interplay that characterises most NaNoGenMo output. It is Whalen's – not the system's – creative vision that is manifest here. Although the exact output of the system cannot be predicted prior to generation, contributing to a sense of computational originality, the system is a tool for realising Whalen's predetermined aesthetic: a humorous (and surprisingly adult-themed) take on a classic children's story. Really, the system produces a textual artefact almost indistinguishable from a human-written book, capitalising upon the conventional codex form (albeit digitised) and engrained linear reading practices. Through *Several Houses'* familiar format, Whalen subtly subverts the textual and visual genre conventions of children's literature, both by satirising a classic nursery rhyme and by quantifying the artistic process so that it is almost entirely randomised. The reader, recognising Whalen's play on conventional children's literature, may appreciate the hilarity of the text itself, but may also appreciate the perceived intention that drove the work's creation more generally, as well as the skill involved in coding the system.

For her 2015 NaNoGenMo submission entitled *Our Arrival: A Novel*, Allison Parrish generated a diary of an expedition through fantastical fictional places. According to the novel's preface (written by Parrish), Parrish's source corpus comprised more than 5,700 sentences from public domain Project Gutenberg books whose subject entries included strings related to the natural sciences, exploration, and science fiction, and whose constructions and content satisfied Parrish's programmed criteria (Parrish, 2015: iii). By parsing and combining randomly selected sentences according to their grammatical constituents, Parrish's system produced a phantasmagorical text that invites readers on a magic carpet ride through the outskirts of the imagination. One entry (Parrish, 2015: 223) reads:

> Large fissures were well wooded as were also those behind.
> They were bent and twisted out of shape.
> You perceived a cradle. It was on the eve of war.
> Discreetly we elected to continue. The roof stood alone in
> the clearing and listened to the diminishing sounds. It had
> the quality of mountains, canyons, and crags.

Although *Our Arrival* is formatted like a typical novel, it is linguistically and topically outside the typical novel's remit. A roof, after all, cannot stand, nor can it listen. And it is remarkably difficult to imagine a roof with the simultaneous qualities of mountains, canyons, and crags. Like Whalen's *Several Houses*, *Our Arrival* subverts the textual conventions of mass-marketed fiction. Syntactically and semantically, it is a textual absurdity that draws one's attention to the potentialities of the linguistic imagination, pushing the boundaries of the usual by repurposing extant texts in the Project Gutenberg corpus. Moreover, both works draw attention to the medium of the book itself. Despite using digital technology not bound to the conventional codex format, both Whalen and Parrish have chosen to present their computer-generated texts in familiar codex forms. Such texts could be seen as bridging a gap between the analogue and the digital, the old and the new, the mundane and the uncharted. Existing within systemic structures of literary convention, readers are guided towards the interpretive processes with which they have grown accustomed through cues of familiar page layouts and intelligible texts.

Despite their similar appearances, though, human-written and computer-generated texts reflect different processes of production. Rather than represent a transition from human-written to computer-generated texts, both Whalen's and Parrish's work testifies to a new kind of text production wherein NLG plays a vital role. Indeed, aesthetic endeavours capitalising on human–computer interplay for text production – *Several Houses* and *Our Arrival* being just two examples – seem a natural step in the evolution of writing technologies, but hardly leave humans obsolete. The computer's involvement need not be limited to wiggly underlines suggesting spelling or grammar changes, but may include participation in the selection of words themselves, influencing – or even determining – the direction of a story. Even in the realm of non-fictional news, this principle holds: to populate human-written templates through programmed instruction is to partake in the process of content curation. The computer is thus an instrument that extends, and fundamentally transforms, the human writing process, though it is still the human developer's vision manifest by means of strict instructions (i.e. algorithms) resulting in profoundly constrained output.

Such output constitutes what one research group from the Dutch Meertens Instituut and the Antwerp Centre for Digital Humanities and Literary Criticism calls 'synthetic literature', resulting from 'co-creativity'

(Manjavacas et al., 2017). In 2017, this group launched the Asibot. Using a graphical user interface, a human author drafts a Dutch-language text, sentence by sentence, with the Asibot proposing sentences to continue the story. To learn language and sentence structure, the system was trained using the texts of 10,000 Dutch e-books. The method of machine learning employed was largely unsupervised, meaning that the system was programmed with basic awareness of global narrative structure but otherwise autonomously distinguished syntactic and semantic patterns within the source corpus. The system also learned how to mimic the unique writing styles of such renowned writers as Isaac Asimov and Dutch novelist Ronald Giphart, and can now generate sentences using similar words and syntax as these writers. Through machine learning the Asibot cultivated its own lived experience of sorts: an experience that, while directed by human instruction, stemmed from particular methods of reading and analysing a body of texts too extensive for any one human to read in a lifetime. This experience enables the Asibot to generate text that adheres to syntactic, semantic, and stylistic convention, while at the same time being sufficiently original.

Giphart himself trialled the Asibot as a co-author for his commission to produce a new story for a Dutch edition of Isaac Asimov's *Ik, robot* that was released specially for the 2017 Nederland Leest campaign. As Giphart typed his own sentences into the interface, the system responded by suggesting numerous sentences to progress the story. Giphart could select one of these suggestions, or ignore the suggestions and continue writing himself. The system's purpose, its developers (Manjavacas et al., 2017: 35) explain, was to 'provoke the human writer in the process of writing.' Giphart himself declared that he still considered himself 'de baas, maar hij doet het werk [the boss, but he (the system) does the work]' (Koolhof, 2017). The system follows its user's direction, but responds by exercising its own programmed creative capacity, derived from its vast knowledge bank amassed through machine learning. Thus, while the other above-mentioned systems were quite clearly tools for actualising individual humans' artistic visions, the Asibot stands in greyer territory. This system can, in a sense, articulate its own lived experiences by drawing from the vast corpora of texts upon which it was trained, its use of language at least somewhat constituting a computational equivalent of cognition. Its contributions may supplement those of the human writer, revealing new avenues for literary traipsing. Alternatively, a human user could choose to accept all of the system's proposals, allowing the system to produce an entire text following from a single inputted prompt. This latter possibility has been the subject of much public deliberation, especially in response to OpenAI's development of their GPT text generators, which effectively operate in such a way (Radford et al., 2019).

4.3 NLG Systems as Agents

It is here where we shift our consideration of NLG systems from being tools for manifesting human vision to viewing them as social agents in themselves (Henrickson, 2018b). Prior to this part of the discussion, it is useful to reflect upon an earlier argument about agency applied to another text-based technology: the printing press. The title of Elizabeth Eisenstein's germinal work about the impact of the printing press is *The Printing Press as an Agent of Change* (1979). Throughout her book, Eisenstein focuses on how the evolution of print coincided with and catalysed widespread cultural changes related to religion, science, and social order. Eisenstein's use of the word 'agent' instead of 'tool' nods to the power of the social structures associated with the printing press over any one individual's use of the technology. Even Gutenberg himself is hardly mentioned. Indeed, the printing press has been not just a tool, but an institution that has transformed social circumstances through new labour economies and processes of text production, dissemination, and reception. Focusing on a technology's large-scale impact rather than singular applications draws attention to that technology's more general social and hermeneutic implications. A printed text does more than just transmit words on a page; it represents an established system of labour and perpetuates the symbolic value of print that constitutes our current Order of the Book. The Order of the Book assigns special significance to books (especially in the printed codex form) because the texts held within those books direct the operation of social institutions (van der Weel, 2011a: 91). It is therefore essential not just to study printed texts as isolated literary artefacts, but to recognise the sociocultural development of these texts, as well as the social and technological developments that have influenced their forms.

So too with computer-generated texts. To appreciate the extent of algorithmic authorship's social and literary impact, it helps to recognise NLG as an agent of change, an institution that transcends any one person or application. There are, of course, some who take issue with Eisenstein's emphasis on a technology as an 'agent' in her discussion of the printing press. One rebuttal by Adriaan van der Weel (2011a: 165) is that 'however important the role of the printing press has been in cultural history, however many genii it may have helped to release from their bottles, it has never – *pace* Elizabeth Eisenstein – been more than a passive instrument in the hands of man.' Van der Weel urges consideration of the printing press as a tool, an augmentation to the human experience through conscious human use. Indeed, the printing press is itself a passive instrument, a tool for actualising human vision. It is the press' output – the printed word – and influence that transforms the press into an agent of change. Put simply, it is not the technology itself that constitutes agency, but its lasting contributions to social transformation. In this way, computational systems may also be regarded as agents of change; the precise nature of change is debatable, but that computational capacity, output, and influence have led to social change is clear. Another rebuttal to Eisenstein's work that explicitly decries her use of the word 'agent' declares that '[a]gents are humans with will, intention and responsibility, while agencies are impersonal: corporations, machines, the weather, gravity. . . . The alternative is to read *agent* figuratively, as a metaphor, more precisely as a personification wherein a thing or abstraction is endowed with life' (Teigen, 1987: 8). In either sense, to deem an NLG system an agent, rather than just a tool, is to acknowledge the wider-ranging social structures associated with algorithmic authorship rather than just NLG's impact on individuals. It is to acknowledge the transformative social power of computer-generated texts. Thus, 'agent' in this Element refers neither to a human with will nor a thing endowed with life. It refers instead to participants in always-mediated processes of communication. 'Agent' refers to someone – or something – that substantially contributes to the creation of output that could be construed as meaningful. 'Agent' refers to someone or something with influence.

Some NLG systems may be regarded as fitting comfortably within the lineage of writing tools, as they quite obviously depend upon embodied figures – humans – for their functionality. For other systems, particularly those wherein the embodied figure is obscured, the distinction between tool and agent is not so clear. If the Asibot were to autonomously generate its own text without Giphart's guidance, could the system still be regarded as a tool? In a machine learning NLG system, at what point is Margaret Boden's assertion of developer responsibility for input determination rendered moot? While some (Bolter, 1991: 189) may argue that in instances of text generation '[t]he computer becomes the author by proxy, in the sense that it operates on the text as the reader reads,' a seemingly disembodied NLG system poses new questions about authorship attribution and how one may negotiate the hermeneutic contract. This is because authorship attribution becomes increasingly complex. The widely held notion that 'computers only do what they are instructed to do', proposed by computing pioneer Ada Lovelace in 1843, still stands (Menabrea, 1843: 722). However, as cognitive scientist Douglas Hofstadter (1980: 306) notes, 'you don't know in advance the consequences of what you tell a computer to do; therefore its behaviour can be as baffling and surprising and unpredictable to you as that of a person. You generally know in advance the *space* in which the output will fall, but you don't know details of where it will fall.' But it is precisely the unpredictability resulting in original content that prompts a shift in perceiving some NLG systems from being mere tools for manifesting human vision to being agents in themselves. Staunch assertions that NLG systems are no more than tools lack recognition of the potential futures of development, and hinder discussions of ethical and social circumstances that may inform judgements of responsibility for system output and claims to financial gain from that output (Prescott, 2017). Agency is what is permitted. The moment a reader begins searching for the intention driving a text's generation is the moment that system is granted agency as a result of a reader's attempt to fulfil the conventional hermeneutic contract. Recognising an NLG system as an agent – and subsequently as an author – welcomes the NLG system into the realm of what Michel Foucault has deemed the 'author function'.

For Foucault, an author's name is not just a description of textual ownership and accountability, but also a designation of which texts are to hold cultural weight. An author's name allows one to classify and define texts in relation to other texts; those texts comprising an author's corpus are seen as complementary, and may be juxtaposed with other corpora. Foucault's author function thus recognises the author as a cultural construct that exists within fluid networks of social circumstances, rather than as any one individual. In Foucault's (1998: 221–2) words, 'the author is not an indefinite source of significations that fill a work; the author does not precede the works; . . . [t]he author is therefore the ideological figure by which one marks the manner in which we fear the proliferation of meaning.'[3] In our world of information abundance, this fear of 'the proliferation of meaning' is increasingly present; the responsibility to make knowledge from information rests increasingly with the reader, who must swim through a sea of non-linear printed works and digital hypertexts that are ever more disembodied from singular human sources. To fear the proliferation of meaning is to fear the responsibility of having to interpret and negotiate the significance of myriad textual artefacts, in either isolation or relation to one another. Linking a text with an author – however imaginary that author may be – streamlines processes of meaning-making, as the reader is not so much faced with a proliferation of meaning within a text, but an expectation that an individual has written with communicative intention. In Foucault's view, the reader's assumption of authorial identity shrouds the subjective nature of reading, contributing to a sense that a text has a 'correct' interpretation rather than full appreciation of that text's contextual malleability.

While writers are physical beings who produce texts, authors are more abstract cultural constructs. In his elaboration upon Foucault's article asking 'What Is an Author?', Alexander Nehamas (1986: 686) explains that writers are 'actual individuals, firmly located in history, efficient causes of their texts.' Authors, however, are 'postulated to account for a text's features and are produced through an interaction between critic and text. Their nature guides interpretation, and interpretation determines their nature. This reciprocal relationship can be called, not simply for a lack of

---

[3] Ironically, as some scholars (Wilson, 2004) have observed, Foucault himself wrestles with the notion of the author as ideological, perhaps due to his own desire for intellectual recognition and celebrity.

a better word, *transcendental*.' Despite its transcendentality, the cultural construct of authorship has very real implications; the common perception of the author as an individual creative genius informs the meaning derived from a text. This perception also informs judicial actions related to the financial and ethical responsibility for a text (Henrickson, 2020). Moreover, Adriaan van der Weel (2015: 2) has argued for a sociotechnical history of authorship, writing that 'the social position of authorship is always founded in a particular sociotechnical constellation of a particular literate mentality and a particular dominant technology for the dissemination of texts.' A text is always a social artefact, created and received by social participants. However, those social participants need not be limited to just human entities. Indeed, social participation may more widely incorporate humans and computers alike, both of which may be considered social agents.

The notion of computers as social participants is more expressly rooted in the Computers Are Social Actors (CASA) paradigm, which holds that humans react similarly to computers as they would to other humans (Nass, Steuer, and Tauber, 1994; Reeves and Nass, 1996). More recent research into users' perceptions of Twitterbots affirms CASA's continued relevance (Spence et al., 2019). Research in robotics supports the CASA paradigm as well (Fischer and Bateman, 2006). In CASA's formative experiments, researchers observed that participants maintained awareness of interacting with computers rather than other humans, but nevertheless extended similar social etiquette (Nass and Moon, 2000). Further, when the experimental computers 'spoke' in different voices, participants responded as through each voice belonged to a distinct entity; participants also applied gender stereotypes to these voices. 'Thus,' these experiments' facilitators (Nass, Steuer, and Tauber, 1994: 77) concluded, 'computer users who respond socially to computers do not feel as though they are interacting with a programmer, but rather attribute socialness directly to the computer itself.' However, while computers could be argued to be social actors in that they prompt subconscious activation of typical social behaviours, computational entities are not wholly comparable to human entities. Although users respond similarly to computers as they would to humans, computers evidently play very different social roles in these situations, leading to altogether different social dynamics.

Actor-network theory (ANT) is useful for exploring such social dynamics. In ANT, everything in the social and natural world exists within fluid relational networks. Actors need not be humans. According to ANT originator Bruno Latour (2005: 71), 'the questions to ask about any agent are simply the following: Does it make a difference in the course of some other agent's action or not? Is there some trial that allows someone to detect this difference?' In Latour's view, an actor is determined more by its effects on other actors than by any intrinsic properties. An actor is determined by its contribution to current contexts. As a result, an actor can never be considered in isolation, as it acts in accordance with the overarching script, the cast alongside, and the audience observing the scene. Its utterances, its realisations of potentialities, must be appropriate to corresponding situations and recipients. While not necessarily spoken, each of these utterances has a resonant effect, modifying the current state of affairs through some sort of detectable difference achieved by interaction with other social entities. Actors have power because other actors have recognised their transformative capacities. Actors create unique environments by virtue of their very existence.

Latour uses the words 'actor' and 'agent' interchangeably, but for the purposes of this discussion it is worth considering these words' differing connotations. An actor performs rehearsed scripts, while agency suggests accountability and intention. Analyses of computational agency have tended to use human agency as a baseline for evaluating the perceived accountability and intention of machines. Some scholars (Johnson, 2006) have suggested alternative phrasing to accommodate the differences between human and computer decision-making processes. Others (Stahl, 2004) have argued for comparative approaches to establish a human–computer dichotomy. Others (Powers, 2013) have argued that computers may one day achieve moral agency by demonstrating phenomenological awareness and intentionality. For all of these scholars, agency is assumed to correspond with the human characteristic of intention that is (arguably) informed by free will.

In John Searle's 'Chinese Room' thought experiment, an individual with no understanding of the Chinese language is locked in a room and given numerous batches of Chinese writing. The individual is then given a set of

English-language rules (a 'program') that correlates pieces of Chinese input with appropriate Chinese responses. Working in this way, the individual produces output indistinguishable from that of native Chinese speakers. Computer programs may similarly manipulate formal symbols without understanding them to produce understandable texts, despite the programs themselves being incapable of free-will intentionality. Nevertheless, in Searle's (1980: 419) words, 'we often attribute "understanding" and other cognitive predicates by metaphor and analogy[.] . . . The reason we make these attributions is quite interesting, and it has to do with the fact that in artifacts we extend our own intentionality; our tools are extensions of our purposes.' As some scholars of algorithmic ethics (Mittelstadt et al., 2016: 10) have observed, though, '[w]hen a technology fails, blame and sanctions must be apportioned. One or more of the technology's designer (or developer), manufacturer or user are typically held accountable. . . . Blame can only be justifiably attributed when the actor has some degree of control . . . and intentionality in carrying out the action.' Focus on text production often centres on intentionality, and Searle himself implies that computers cannot be anything more than tools because they are incapable of the intentionality demonstrated by humans. Given that natural languages are humans' primary means for interpersonal communication, it is reasonable to assume that those who communicate through natural language are doing so to fulfil some communicative goal. Searle's 'human program', producing Chinese texts without understanding the language, may not have so pointed a communicative goal, and may therefore be considered to lack the assumed free-will intentionality of conventional authorial agents.

Expectations of human-specific free-will intentionality have also informed policy discussions related to authorial credit. In the United States' 1979 *Final Report of the National Commission on New Technology Uses of Copyrighted Works* (CONTU Final Report), Commissioner John Hersey declares that 'a definite danger to the quality of life must come with a blurring and merging of human and mechanical communication' (National Commission on New Technological Uses of Copyrighted Works, 1979: 36–7). He argues that one must not equate human beings and machines because:

machines may be able in some distant future to linguistically 'understand' but will never be able to experience, never be able to bring to life, never be able therefore to communicate. Those aspects include courage, love, integrity, trust, the touch of flesh, the fire of intuition, the yearning and aspirations of what poets so vaguely but so persistently call the soul – the bundle of qualities we think of as being embraced by the word humanity.

In Hersey's view, empathy – rather than linguistic capacity – distinguishes human writers from NLG systems. Empathy (and, in turn, the 'soul') establishes textual value, appealing to human readers who too exhibit empathy. Extending this argument, the CONTU Final Report stresses that the computer is incapable of consciously intending communicative meaning; computers are considered tools for manifesting human vision, and do not wield their own intention. The Report (National Commission on New Technological Uses of Copyrighted Works, 1979: 45) summarises this argument thus: 'Computers are enormously complex and powerful instruments which vastly extend human powers to calculate, select, rearrange, display, design and do other things involved in the creation of works. However, it is a human power they extend.' The human power extended is implied to be one of free-will intentionality.

An argument for computational agency questions this focus on the assumed free-will intentionality of authorial agents by following from Daniel Dennett's notion of the 'intentional stance'. Through the intentional stance, the behaviour of an actor - and by extension an agent - is interpreted by considering its beliefs and desires (Dennett, 1971). When faced with an entity – whether human or not – we assume rational behaviour appropriate to the relevant social circumstances. We therefore ascribe beliefs and desires to that entity. Dennett uses a chess-playing computer as an illustration. 'Lingering doubts about whether the chess-playing computer *really* has beliefs and desires are misplaced,' he writes (Dennett, 1971: 91), 'and whether one calls what one ascribes to the computer beliefs or belief-analogues or information complexes or Intentional whatnots makes no difference to the nature of the calculation one makes on the basis of the ascriptions.' Nevertheless:

> We do quite successfully treat these computers as
> Intentional systems, and we do this independently of any
> considerations about what substance they are composed of,
> their origin, their position or lack of position in the com-
> munity of moral agents, their consciousness or self-
> consciousness, or the determinacy or indeterminacy of
> their operations.

For Dennett, users' perceptions of systems are more significant than actual
system functionality. Following from ANT, if users ascribe beliefs and
desires to a system, thereby welcoming the system into a social network,
that system becomes a social agent. In one example of the intentional stance,
Dennett considers a thermostat. One may regard a thermostat as a mere
control mechanism for regulating temperature, whose regulatory functionality may be applied to myriad situations (e.g. a car's cruise control). The
thermostat's technology is not constrained to any one boiler, or even to the
domain of temperature. However, the more the thermostat is integrated into
the world – the more complex its internal operations become as a result of
enriched connections with other entities associated with its assigned task
(e.g. the thermostat purchases its own boiler fuel or checks a house's
weather stripping) – the more one can say that the thermostat 'has beliefs
about heat and *about this very room*, and so forth, not only because of the
system's actual location in, and operations on, the world, but because we
cannot imagine another niche in which it could be placed *where it would
work*' (Dennett, 1987: 31). The thermostat becomes a distinctive agent that
fulfils a certain social function, prompting the emergence of new organisations of behaviour and thought that centre on the thermostat. David
Herman's (2008: 257) more recent consideration of the intentional stance
applies it to narrative theory, concluding that 'stories simultaneously reflect
and activate a disposition to adopt the intentional stance.' Connecting
Dennett's notion of the intentional stance with more recent developments
in AI and algorithmic authorship, there are efforts in the field of explainable
AI/explainable computational intelligence to enable machine learning systems to describe their decision-making processes, often in natural languages, and these descriptions may support a sense of autonomous

computational intentionality. Such systems stimulate reorganisations of behaviour and thought motivated by efforts to understand computational decisions. An NLG system may not just reflect human beliefs, but may be regarded as having beliefs of its own because it becomes a distinctive entity that fulfils a certain social function resulting in original output. These beliefs are not necessarily rooted in free-will intentionality. Many systems exercise forms of intentionality not governed by free will, but by efforts to fulfil designated objectives, like Searle's human program. Systems become social agents by contributing to and transforming social networks.

Such scrutiny of semantics may seem pedantic, but in a discussion of NLG systems the recognition of computational agency is imperative for complete understanding of these systems' roles within contemporary circumstances. Regardless of whether an author is a human or a computer, the reader's process of meaning-making is fundamentally the same: fashion a narrative about authorial intention. As Katherine Hayles notes in her book about *Digital Subjects and Literary Texts* (2005: 197) when discussing the attribution of motives and intentions related to texts, 'narratives allow us to construct models of how others may be feeling and acting, models that coevolve with our ongoing interior monologues describing and interpreting to ourselves our own feelings and behaviors.' Writing about computer-generated texts in particular, Manuel Portela (2018: 195) notes that '[e]ven if there is a certain degree of mathematical randomness in the verbal output, linguistic combinations will have emergent meanings that will be read literally. Random textual instantiations thus open up machinic constraints to the unconscious of the reader.' All this is to say that the narrative text – in this case a computer-generated text – prompts the production of another narrative *about* that text within the readerly mind. The reader seeks authorial intention through engagement with engrained hermeneutic processes, fulfilling Dennett's intentional stance. If a reader who did understand Chinese were to read the text produced by Searle's human program, for example, that reader would still consider the text in light of the assumed intentionality of an imagined authorial agent. We legitimise our lived experiences to ourselves and others by using natural language, and the use of natural language alone is enough to provoke instinctual ascribing of beliefs and desires to an imagined author so as to discern the assumed communicative function of a text. The NLG system's use of natural language therefore immediately distinguishes it as being on the figurative border between tool and agent. The computer may be used to alter the current state of affairs through an 'actor' role, as in Whalen's *Several Houses* NaNoGenMo submission, wherein the computer was employed as a tool. Much algorithmically authored output, however, situates the computer within the realm of 'agent' as a result of the social power assigned to it, however unconsciously, once a reader attempts to discern the communicative function of output by imagining an author. This is a question of social, rather than moral, agency.

It is this permitted agency that links Dennett's intentional stance to the hermeneutic contract. Recall that the hermeneutic contract refers to the relationship between the reader and the author. It rests on two assumptions: that readers believe that authors want them to be interested in their texts, and that authors want readers to understand their texts. To fulfil this contract, however, the reader must assign beliefs and desires to the disembodied author. As discussed in Section 3, the modern notion of 'author' tends towards understanding the author as an individual creative genius, imagined as per a 'cult of personality'. Yet, to cite NLG system developer Jean-Pierre Balpe (1995: 24 [translation my own]), if 'computer literature is literally readable, then it is radically positioned outside of this "classical" literary ideology wherein a master of letters has reigned for centuries: no inspiration or original experience, no intention or genius . . . no authorial individuality.' Regardless of whether the author is a human or non-human entity, the reader infers the intentions of an imagined and disembodied author based on a process of meaning-making that rests upon the assumption of mutual understanding through shared sociocultural traditions. To investigate intention by necessity assumes agency. It is therefore not enough to merely say that NLG systems are tools, or even social actors. They are social agents, because readers treat them as such.

4.4 Algorithmic Authorship and the Hermeneutic Contract

Readers are rarely given detailed information about processes of computer-generated text production. However, the results of a recent series of studies exploring how authorship is attributed to computer-generated texts indicate that readers often identify NLG systems as authors (Henrickson, 2019a/b). After all, when one reads the final *Ik, robot* story co-produced by Ronald Giphart and the Asibot, one cannot distinguish which parts of the texts have come from Giphart and which have come from the system. The collaboration between human and computer has resulted in a seamless 'synthetic literature' that reflects both Giphart's and the Asibot's lived experiences and intentions, as well as their relationships with one another. There are two, rather than one, sources of communicative intention: Giphart, in corporal form; and the Asibot, in computational form. Giphart's intentions may reflect the free will that is presumed of human individuals. The Asibot's intentions, though, may constitute a wholly different kind of intention: one characterised by efforts to fulfil designated objectives through processing and repurposing Dutch-language e-books for the production of sufficiently original content. The distinction between these two forms of intention permits more nuanced consideration of the ways in which algorithmic authorship may contribute to textual landscapes. The Asibot's – and, more generally, the algorithmic author's – power is exerted throughout the co-creative process and is affirmed the moment a reader begins interpreting its output. The writing system, human writer, and readers exist within a fluid network of social relationships rooted in reciprocal exchanges related to power, whether explicitly or implicitly acknowledged. This is not to neglect the important questions of moral, financial, and legal responsibility for textual content. Recognising an NLG system as a social agent does not automatically make that system solely responsible for its output; questions of responsibility are still to be sufficiently pondered. Recognising an NLG system as a social agent, though, does allow for the situation of NLG within a lineage of textual technologies and literary studies. Readers consider computer-generated output in light of their expectations for human-written texts. 'When faced with a totally new situation,' Marshall McLuhan (with Fiore and Agel, 1967: 74) writes, 'we tend always to attach ourselves to the objects, to the flavor of the most recent past. We look at the present through a rear-view mirror. We march backwards into the future.'

Computer-generated texts bring conventional understandings of the author–reader relationship – what I have called the hermeneutic contract – into question. The author of a computer-generated text is ambiguous:

potentially human, potentially computational. Nevertheless, the understanding of texts as being of social – interpersonal, *human* – value persists. Computer-generated texts not only appeal to readers' expectations of textual authority simply by virtue of being natural language text, but also by mimicking the familiar forms of the printed word. Despite computer-generated and human-written texts often being indistinguishable, though, the two means of text production are decidedly different. This is why it is not enough to consider the implications of NLG systems based on output alone. In McLuhan's words:

> All media work us over completely. They are so pervasive
> in their personal, political, economic, aesthetic, psychologi-
> cal, moral, ethical, and social consequences that they leave
> no part of us untouched, unaffected, unaltered. The medium
> is the massage. Any understanding of social and cultural
> change is impossible without a knowledge of the way media
> work as environments. All media are extensions of some
> human faculty – psychic or physical (McLuhan, Fiore, and
> Agel, 1967: 26).

To appreciate the extent of algorithmic authorship's sociocultural impact, one must consider the unique labour economies and social infrastructures spurred by NLG. Although recent discussions about computer-generated texts have focused primarily on whether computer-generated texts can pass the Turing test – whether a human reader can be tricked into believing that a computer-generated text has been written by a human – such a measure only evaluates final linguistic output and does not appraise computational thought, intelligence, or intentionality. New technologies like NLG prompt renegotiation of the self and the self in relation to society, encouraging reassessment of human roles in established processes of production and reception. Arguably, the Turing test standard detracts from the more important issue of determining algorithmic authorship's place within the current sociocultural and literary climates. It detracts from attention to the human experiences of computer-generated texts.

It is through language that interpersonal agency is exercised, and the hermeneutic contract is rooted in the reader's expectation of authorial agency that is informed by lived experience. Texts are perceived as products of human self-expression. Of course, genre may also inform one's expectations of textual content. This is why, for example, Zach Whalen's *The Several Houses of Brian, Spencer, Liam, Victoria, Brayden, Vincent, and Alex* is recognisable as a piece of children's literature, despite its occasional adult themes and jumbled illustrations. The reader reads according to the constraints of the customary. Still, though, it is the reader who establishes and maintains the hermeneutic contract through acts of interpretation, and the hermeneutic contract stands regardless of genre; it simply holds that texts are understood as having been produced from communicational intention. What is more, interpretation, in Alexander Nehamas' (1986: 688) words, 'places a text within a perpetually broadening context, not within a continually deepening one. . . . Interpretation ends when interest wanes, not when certainty, or an ultimate meaning, is reached.' A reader may regard a text as the product of authorial intention, but it is the reader who actually determines what a text means.

So, how important is recognition of authorial intention for textual interpretation? This question has long been debated by literary critics, who have cycled between tendencies towards authorial intention (e.g. biographical criticism), and then towards reader experience (e.g. New Criticism). Writing from a perspective informed by both book history and textual scholarship, Peter Shillingsburg (2006: 55–6) explores the ambiguous nature of intention. '[N]o matter how radical one's objection is to the concept of intention as a controlling element of textual interpretation, some aspect of intention by some agent of intention is inescapable in any reading act,' Shillingsburg writes. '[R]eaders knowingly or blindly participate in a negotiation over authority in script acts, finding or inventing concepts of authorship and intention, which they then ignore or flout or seek to embrace.' The hermeneutic contract recognises the complex negotiations that occur within the reader to discern authorial intention while still establishing one's own interpretation of the text under consideration. There is, of course, the reader's expectation of the text as something intended to be understandable and interesting or, in some instances, intentionally incomprehensible or dull for aesthetic purposes. Texts are not simply aesthetic artefacts, though. They are embedded with communicative function and, as

Shillingsburg rightly observes, the precise ways readers may negotiate this communicative function are not so easily anticipated. One oft-referenced stance is the 'death of the author': Roland Barthes' 1967 argument that attributing an author to a text constrains its readers' interpretations of that text given an assumption that there is one definitive meaning established by the writer. Barthes (1977: 148) explains that '[c]lassic criticism has never paid any attention to the reader; for it, the writer is the only person in literature. ... [W]e know that to give writing its future, it is necessary to overthrow the myth: the birth of the reader must be at the cost of the death of the Author.' But although the printed word is an artefact largely disembodied from its initial writer through the mechanised and communal processes of its production, the sense of authorial intention is an integral part of its legitimacy. As a reader reads, she interprets a text in light of an assumed communicational intention informed by a commitment to mutual understanding that itself is informed by shared sociocultural traditions and appropriate language usage. Whether the reader chooses to accept what she believes was the author's intention during writing, or whether she chooses to disregard it, meaning is discerned through attention to intention. To reiterate Shillingsburg, the reader consciously or unconsciously negotiates a text's authority, choosing to succumb to or ignore perceived authorial intention. The author is not dead, but imagined. And the author is important, for it is in relation to the author that the reader makes meaning. It matters little whether the author is human or algorithmic; the reader continues to search for meaning.

Section 3 argued that algorithmic authorship extends the current societal trend towards what I have called 'hyper-individualism'. Hyper-individualism refers to each individual's tendency towards self-gratification, driven by senses of self-importance and uniqueness. Through individualism, each seeks personalisation through subjective curation of media; through hyper-individualism, personalisation is pervasive in both analogue and digital forms. While media may still be curated by individuals, curation is now subject to algorithmic filters that are both conspicuous and concealed. A comprehensive analysis of computer-generated texts must therefore account not only for the author function, but also the unique functions of the reader and the text itself in light of the proliferation of non-experts: ordinary people reading and interpreting texts, who may have limited knowledge of these texts' production processes. Hyper-individualism not only legitimises an individual's sense of self, but also supports fragmented processes of meaning-making wherein the interpretive burden rests ever more with the reader rather than with the author as a result of algorithmic ubiquity.

Hyper-individualism is magnified by the rise of companies that specialise in the generation of news articles for consumption by general and niche audiences alike. When transforming datasets (e.g. sports scores, weather forecasts, stock performances) into readable narratives, these companies' systems demonstrate the capacity to rapidly generate texts that are highly personalised in both content and register. Computer-generated texts may therefore appear disembodied from their producers, but find embodiment within the readers for whom they were generated. Readers not only consume relevant knowledge, but help create it. Even for non-personalised computer-generated texts the individualism of the reader is affirmed, if only because there is no longer an obvious author to whom one may attribute authorship and, by extension, intention. The author function blurs.

Attention to readers' documented experiences of computer-generated texts is especially important given that some NLG systems have begun producing altogether new kinds of literature: literature that may not conform to the syntactic and semantic conventions to which readers have grown accustomed. Considering one of the short stories in Racter's 1984 *The Policeman's Beard is Half Constructed*, marketed as 'the first book ever written by a computer', *Scientific American* writer A. K. Dewdney (1985: 10) writes:

> Even a layperson may have concluded that Racter is decidedly schizophrenic. On the one hand, the ideas brought together in these sentences seem to form a coherent whole. It is nice that Sarah and Bill sing to each other. Although I had not thought of singing as dangerous, I am positively charmed by the idea of the two eating lamb, stroking each other and chanting about their ups and downs. On the other

hand, the allowances I have been making for Racter all along are stretched to the breaking point when Racter mentions that besides their love they also have typewriters. Invited to share in this extraordinary insight, I tremble on the brink of a completely unknown mental world, one that I would prefer not to enter.

Racter's syntactic bumbling, jumping from one topic to another, often with no logical connections between topics, leaves Dewdney with the sense that he is reading the work of an author unhinged. Nevertheless, Dewdney acknowledges the 'extraordinary insight' that this output might offer him, despite his reluctance to enter into the computational writer's mind.

In another review of computer-generated text, Charles Hartman (1996: 71) recounts his experiences developing a poetry generation system, explaining why the output of his AutoPoet could not be deemed a 'victory'. For context, the AutoPoet generated such output as:

> The garden of steel – place – had figured in
> this. When I am every afternoon,
> how can't the last teacher write? But I
> was art without my play between a result
> and the metabolism, and the night
> of language toward a story between the part
> and any light (the thin subject) remains.

And so forth. Hartman (1996: 72) reflects:

> AutoPoet embodied an inappropriate idea of poetry. As long as the goal was the imitation of a human poet – or as long as the poem's reader was encouraged to think that was the goal – I wasn't likely to get any farther. What's wrong with the AutoPoetry I've quoted here (and all the other reams of it the machine would produce until it was turned off) is exactly that it's *imitation poetry*. All our habits of reading are called upon, all the old expectations, and then let

> down. 'Monologues of Soul and Body' [another one of
> Hartman's computer-generated poems] had worked because
> its 'body' sections were so *different* from human poetry. It
> had successfully demanded its own way of reading.

'All our habits of reading are called upon, all the old expectations, and then let down,' Hartman declares. However, this Element, supported by a series of empirical studies investigating reader responses to computer-generated texts (Henrickson, 2019a/b), shows that these expectations are not let down. Readers continue to engage in processes of meaning-making when faced with computer-generated texts, however dull or nonsensical those texts may be. Readers continue to imagine the author, even for a computer-generated text, because they instinctually aim to fulfil the hermeneutic contract to which they are accustomed. Although Hartman believes his AutoPoet failed because it did not sufficiently draw from its own lived experiences and emotional perceptions to produce truly 'unique' work, the only expectations that are actually let down are those of Hartman himself.

All the same, the expectation for computer-generated texts that pass the Turing test is pervasive amongst those considering algorithmic authorship. Underlying such an expectation is an assumption that the end goal of an NLG system is not to generate output that is unique in its own right, but output that can deceive human readers into believing that it has been human-written. Martin Eve (2017: 46) reflects upon an RNN he trained to generate textual output that mimics the writing style of articles from the literary studies journal *Textual Practice*: 'the network has no motivation towards communication and no epistemological goal except to achieve ever more perfection in its stylistic mimicry of the articles in *Textual Practice*.' Despite the RNN producing text that is understandable, albeit verbose, Eve is unwilling to call the system an 'author'. He calls the proliferation of NLG systems 'alarming', not only because these systems threaten to wholly mechanise current labour practices, but also because he believes that they depreciate narrative quality and undermine the work of narrative scholars. According to Eve (2017: 51):

> [I]n achieving a mimesis of human writing – remember, a measure of intelligence formed only by anthropocentric reference to the human – computational writing asks us to imagine a world in which there are no more humans undertaking such labour. Such thinking only emerges, though, in the imagined substitution of the human with human-like automata. This imagined world is both a post-anthropocentric world for writers and a world in which a writing machine that is legitimated by human-like characteristics is inscribed at the centre. It is concurrently a world in which we have no benchmark of contemporary writing success, but one that is nonetheless dominated by machines that meet that nostalgic target.

Eve's hypothetical world exemplifies an approach to thinking about computer-generated texts that tends towards apocalyptic outcomes for human labour because computers can produce adequate imitations of human-written texts. Reviewing Racter's *The Policeman's Beard* nearly two decades after its publication, experimental writer Christian Bök (2002: 10) more bluntly writes that 'RACTER is a mindless identity, whose very acephalia [absence of a head] demonstrates the fundamental irrelevance of the writing subject in the manufacture of the written product. The involvement of an author in the production of literature has henceforth become discretionary.' Similarly, novelist and critic Steve Tomasula (2018: 50) has argued that computer-generated texts exemplify a kind of 'postliterary literature' that 'is informed by an accompanying posthuman ethos – one that is at odds with an ethos based upon the uniqueness of the individual, and its cousins, especially originality.' But an algorithmic author does not ask us to imagine a world in which there are no more humans undertaking textual labour. It simply prompts us to imagine a world in which algorithmic authorship has a place alongside human authorship. It encourages us to adapt to the new circumstances of an increasingly digital age. And, most importantly, NLG systems may produce different kinds of texts altogether: ones that challenge readers' syntactic and semantic expectations and demand their own interpretive approaches. As a result, value judgements about system output are impractical at this time. As new genres emerge, it is more appropriate simply to observe creators – both corporal and computational – as they explore the new social and literary potentialities permitted by algorithmic authorship. This Element has aimed to start a discussion about how modern conceptions of authorship and reader responsibility apply to instances of computer-generated texts. Once this foundation has been established, judgements of literary value – as well as the perceived extent and value of authorial intention – may be of greater relevance.

4.5 Conclusion

Disembodied from the text, save for perhaps an accompanying name, the author has long been imagined by the reader through participation in the hermeneutic contract. For computer-generated texts, though, the author is not so clear a figure, not so easily personified through consideration of linguistic tone or perceived interpersonal connection. Yet the reader's assumption of the conventional hermeneutic contract continues to inform the reading experience, and the NLG system is evaluated through comparison to the human writer. When a system produces output that exists alongside human-written text, readers may interpret this output as reflecting the same commitment to adhere to and perpetuate shared sociocultural traditions as that presumed of a human writer: in such instances, these are the traditions of appropriate semantic and syntactic structures. In this way, the NLG system itself takes on a fundamentally social role distinct from that of its developers. It stands on the fence between tool and agent, teetering ever closer to the realm of agency that characterises modern conceptions of authorship. Recognising NLG systems as agents in themselves, as social institutions with transformative power rather than mere tools for actualising human vision, serves to counteract comparisons of NLG systems to human writers, permitting clearer recognition of the unique contributions of algorithmic authorship to the social and literary landscapes. The type of agency exerted by these systems need not be characterised by the free-will intention of human writers, but may instead be characterised by the programmed intention to fulfil a designated objective that is respected within wider social networks: a deterministic approach to being, so to speak. Algorithmic authorship necessitates new infrastructures of text production and dissemination, but also necessitates new infrastructures of thought. Computer-generated texts necessitate a new literacy that helps us make sense of digital methods of text production and articulate our own human experiences and interpretations using digital media. This is a literacy that more explicitly recognises the reader's responsibility for making meaning. The hermeneutic contract maintains its relevance, but only as a starting point for fuller understanding of algorithmic authorship's implications achieved through a sociology of computer-generated texts.

A call to recognise NLG systems as agents in themselves does not negate the fundamentally human facets of text production and interpretation. Computer-generated texts – like human-written texts – always emerge from, and function within the confines of, human vision. Systems are developed according to developers' objectives, and texts are read with expectations of underlying communicational intention. Texts have no inherent meaning, but are assigned meaning by human writers and readers. Further, computational agency complements human agency, facilitating new methods of exploring and articulating human experience. NLG systems augment the speed and power of human capacities for text production, extending human faculties. While they may take the place of some human writers, they remain dependent upon humans for their functionality, operation, and maintenance. They contribute to new sociologies of text, offering alternative textual performances wherein the reader's experience is prioritised over that of the author. Acknowledging NLG systems as agents rather than mere tools prompts reflection upon the distinct labour economies driving and emerging from algorithmic authorship. Such acknowledgement facilitates recognition of the transformative social power of system output, contributing to more nuanced discussions of how algorithmic authorship conforms to and/or confronts conventional author–reader relationships.

And so we return to Amersfoort, in de Bibliotheek Eemland. A robot arm lifts a copy of the new edition of *Ik, robot*, passing it to a man with an advanced prosthetic hand: a cyborg. The cyborg then passes the book to the human, who raises it for the audience to see. The crowd cheers, excited to read the synthetic literature that is the product of human–computer collaboration. NLG systems such as those used to write a new story for *Ik, robot* may be equated with puppets, generating output according to specific instructions, but their implications for authorship make them something more. These systems represent a new literary institution wherein the human author is overcome by a computational entity, and the reader is at the forefront of meaning-making. Of course, reading is never a passive act, and it never has been. In instances of computer-generated texts, though, the reader builds upon computational output to (co-)create knowledge from information, to embed texts with meaning and social relevance. Through human–computer synthesis, a text is generated according to appropriate literary structures. By employing language from which readers derive meaning, the NLG system becomes a social agent in itself. It is an agent of change.

5 Conclusion

Let us now revisit Simon, sitting in his local café with his newspaper set down on the table in front of him. 'Majority of New Mothers in Wolverhampton Are Unmarried' (Anon., 2017) reads the title of one story. Rather than being written by a human, though, this story has been computer-generated by a company called Urbs Media, which boasts its technological power for 'crafting stories and harnessing automation to mass localise' (Urbs Media). *Now I feel like I'm on the set of a sci-fi film*, Simon thinks to himself.

Despite sounding science-fictional, computer-generated texts abound. Data-driven news articles like Simon's 'Majority of New Mothers' are common applications of NLG. However, as has been shown throughout this Element, news is only one of NLG's many domains. Machines are generating texts for expository and aesthetic purposes, and have been doing so for more than a century.

Computer-generated texts in their current forms, however, bring modern conventions into question. In our current state – the Order of the Book – books (especially tangible codices) are assigned symbolic value because the texts contained within them direct the operation of social institutions that sustain modern representative democracy and perpetuate cultural and literary heritage (van der Weel, 2011a: 91). The Order of the Book is characterised by social institutions of authorship and widely held understandings of reader responsibility for interpreting messages that authors have explicitly and implicitly embedded within their texts. Yet as van der Weel (2011a: 178) observes, the 'interpretive burden' rests increasingly with the reader, as digital-born texts challenge the standardisation and linearity of the mass-printed word. Left to make sense of an abundance of available texts, the reader is put in a state of privilege that emerges from and supports a cultural tendency towards hyper-individualism: an exaggerated understanding of the reader as meaning-maker. NLG augments hyper-individualism through its ability to mass-generate highly localised texts in short periods of time. One example of a highly localised text is Simon's 'Majority of New Mothers' article, which reports statistics specific to Wolverhampton. In more extreme cases, individual readers are presented with narratives produced just for them, affirming their senses of self within an age of information overload that may otherwise seem stifling to any one voice. Although the Order of the Book is challenged by the sheer proliferation of texts that permit hyper-individualised reading, NLG developers capitalise upon ingrained assumptions of textual and codicological value.

Computer-generated texts represent today's digital ecology, transforming what has largely been seen as an extension of the human self – text, the claim to authorship – into an esoteric entanglement of human and computer involvements. Ultimately, NLG is about computational choice and creativity. According to its programmed instructions, the system must choose what content to include in its output, and how to convey selected output. By applying a sociological perspective to an analysis of computer-generated texts, though, we can see these texts more clearly for what they are: human artefacts, produced by humans for human reception. These artefacts have notable implications for the social and literary spheres, with one of the most significant but implicit being that they bring into question the conventional imagined relationship – the hermeneutic contract – between reader and author. I have therefore argued for a semantic shift from the NLG system as tool to the system as agent, based on a broader understanding of agency as defined by both free-will and programmed forms of intentionality. The NLG system holds social power because readers attempt to derive meaning from its output. The NLG system is a communicative medium with the ability to transform social circumstances with its output, and even its very presence. It has social agency; it is a social agent; it truly becomes an algorithmic author.

In conversation at the Electronic Literature Organization's 2018 conference, one artist whose practice centres on producing computer-generated text solicited advice.[4] 'When my work does get press,' she explained, 'the output is often attributed to my bots, rather than to me. But *I* am the one who creates. How do I make sure I am the one being given credit?' This leads to what are possibly the most important questions arising from this discussion, which have gone unaddressed until this point. What are we to do with this theorising? How do we want readers to respond to these

---

[4] Anonymised poet, conversation with the author (15 August 2018, Montreal).

works? Can developers of NLG systems guide readers towards desired responses? How do different genres of computer-generated texts – news articles and poems, for example – demand different kinds of interpretive responses or authorship attributions? What does accepting an NLG system as a social agent mean for literary analysis of both expository and aesthetic texts? It is beyond the scope of this Element to provide such answers, and the responsibility lies with future research projects involving both scholars and system developers to settle on answers that are rooted in nuanced understandings of where computer-generated texts fit within current circumstances. As computer-generated texts become increasingly present in our everyday lives, these are questions that demand urgent consideration. The answers to such questions will inform the bot-making artist's practice and journalistic approaches to authorship attribution.

Indeed, studies about the social implications of algorithmic authorship are nearly non-existent. Discussions about NLG have been dominated by computer scientists driving system development, and often focus on evaluating the functionality of systems using computational and empirical methods; functionality is more often than not defined by a system's ability to deceive users into believing its output has been human-written. The preceding pages represent an effort to begin filling this gap by discerning the social implications of algorithmic authorship and establishing a theoretical foundation for further studies. This effort was channelled by situating NLG's lineage and current applications within greater historical contexts related to the effects of technological development on communications media. Despite uncertainty about this technology, NLG is only becoming more prominent in the modern textual landscape, which itself is ever-changing and subject to cartographic subjectivity.

The social, hermeneutic, and literary implications of algorithmic authorship are vast, and research incorporating scholars from the humanities, the social sciences, computer science, and other academic fields and industrial areas is needed to fully comprehend the implications of this textual phenomenon. As Dennis Tenen writes in his book *The Poetics of Computation* (2017: 199), '[t]echnologies that govern literacy cannot be allowed to develop apart from the humanities. Such detachment threatens the legacy of interpretive practice, enacted on page or pacemaker. Whatever their politics, literary scholars, philosophers, and historians must negotiate the tactics of reading alongside lawmakers and software engineers.' Tenen advocates interdisciplinary collaboration to negotiate how technologies may create, reinforce, and subvert hierarchical systems of social governance privileging a technocratic elite. This Element has set the groundwork for such negotiations as they pertain to algorithmic authorship. Starting from the broad base established herein, future research can approach the world of computer-generated texts with narrower scopes that explore more pointed research aims and objectives.

Future studies, for example, could place greater emphasis on the exegetical experiences provoked by computer-generated texts, more precisely delineating readers' processes of making meaning from computational output. Such studies may incorporate literary analyses of these texts, exploring the stylistic elements of computer-generated texts that influence conscious and unconscious processes of interpretation. They may draw from the scholarship about electronic literature – works where the digital not only supports the writing process, but plays an integral part in a text's development and reception – as such scholarship has largely focused on the literary merits of specific texts, with occasional investigations into the phenomenological experiences of readers engaging with them. Future studies may also benefit by drawing from the field of affective NLG, which is defined by its efforts to evoke emotional responses in readers through conscious employment of words and sentence structures. However, the well of empirical studies related to affective NLG and the aesthetic experiences prompted by computer-generated output is remarkably shallow, and has been largely untouched by researchers outside of computer science. Supplemented by a team that incorporates the electronic literature community and affective NLG researchers, humanities researchers are especially well suited to catalyse this area of study, given their attention to the subtle ways language may be used for persuasion, entertainment, and aesthetic purposes. By integrating these disciplines' quantitative and qualitative tendencies, respectively, a deeper understanding of NLG's potential for overcoming common perceptions of mechanised impassivity may be realised.

Humanities researchers are also well suited to scrutinising the metaphors both developers and ordinary readers use to talk about NLG systems. The humanities have long been attuned to the ways in which metaphor reflects and shapes perceptions of the world, and close attention to perceptions as they are manifest through language may reveal more tacit understandings of algorithmic authorship. Metaphor may be helpful in positioning algorithmic authorship within the current cultural climate, but may also impede full comprehension of technological capability. Further, different groups – ordinary readers and developers, for example – may use different metaphors aligned with their respective frames of reference. On a practical level, though, understanding – and capitalising upon – the metaphors ordinary readers already use to conceptualise algorithmic authorship may contribute to more effective descriptions of systems that apply user-friendly metaphors instead of more potentially confusing developer-driven ones. On a more theoretical level, investigation into the metaphors that ordinary readers use may promote deeper understanding of attitudes towards algorithmic authorship, whether they be positive, negative, or (as I predict) altogether uncertain. Literary scholars are especially well equipped for this task.

Future studies could also shift the focus from the reader – who was paramount here – to the developer, investigating intention expressed throughout development, as well as distinguishing the underlying assumptions that inform a system's course of development. Such studies may benefit from formal qualitative and quantitative research, as well as from less formal observations of development team meetings and interviews with individual developers. Working with development communities would undoubtedly reveal entirely different perspectives on the social and hermeneutic implications of algorithmic authorship: perspectives that may affirm, contradict, or add nuance to those of ordinary readers, contributing to more holistic understandings of algorithmic authorship's place in the modern world.

Similarly, examination of different language groups' responses to computer-generated texts may lead to alternative conclusions. The French-speaking world, for example, has become deeply familiar with experimental literature driven by systematic production. The Oulipo movement, ongoing since 1960, has prompted academic and popular discussion about text-production processes; the published proceedings of a 1994 conference in Paris (Vuillemin and Lenoble, 1995) show that the French have long been discussing questions of authorship as they pertain to computer-generated texts, albeit only occasionally. As described in Section 4, the Dutch-speaking world recently saw the release of a new edition of Isaac Asimov's *Ik, robot* (*I, Robot*) that featured a new story co-produced by an NLG system; the sense of excitement at this book's launch event suggested generally positive reception of a computer-generated text. The distinct literary traditions of different language groups may inform these groups' responses to algorithmic authorship, and may even contribute to deeper appreciation of computer-generated texts on the part of readers from these groups. Language idiosyncrasies may also impact speakers' uses of metaphor to conceptualise algorithmic authorship.

There are also avenues for future studies of algorithmic authorship within the domain of ethics. As NLG systems are developed to be increasingly autonomous, exploration of the potential ethical quandaries posed by the proposed treatment of NLG systems as social agents – rather than just tools for manifesting human creative vision – will become paramount. How is remuneration to be paid to a computer system that (currently) has no financial interest? If no payment is necessary, how are the economic structures of publishing affected? Who is to be held accountable for offensive or inaccurate texts when those texts have been generated by seemingly autonomous systems? A discussion of whether AI systems and robots ought to be afforded moral agency is already underway (Bryson, 2018). This discussion, however, has hardly been extended to text production, and there has been virtually no scholarly or industrial consideration of the effects of computer-generated texts on the current architectures of the publishing industry aside from some legal deliberations about copyright law and intellectual property. Recognising an NLG system as a social agent does not make that system morally, financially, or legally responsible for its output; it simply serves as a starting point for recognising the unique contributions NLG systems can make to text production. Questions about the authorial responsibility for computer-generated texts have yet to be sufficiently pondered, despite attempts by such bodies as the United States' 1970s Commission on New Technology Uses of Copyrighted Work to negotiate where computer-generated works fit within contemporary conceptions of copyright. These are discussions that must be revisited by scholars in more judicially minded fields, as well as by social scientists and humanities scholars with eyes that are trained to navigate through murky grey areas.

Finally, Section 4's argument for the consideration of NLG systems as social agents may be extended to systems that produce computer-generated music, visual art, or other kinds of output typically regarded as manifestations of human communicational intention and/or creativity. These discussions have already begun, but may benefit from the incorporation of that which has been argued here.

We have long been at a point at which systems are generating texts that are indistinguishable from those written by humans. In recent years, however, algorithmic authorship has become ever more pervasive in the everyday lives of ordinary readers. Computer-generated news articles and business reports hold increasing power to inform readers' understandings of themselves and the world around them. Whether a personalised audit report (with the help of Narrative Science), a bespoke book-length report about *Facial Tissue Stock Excluding Toweling, Napkin, and Toilet Paper* (à la Philip Parker), or a 50,000-word 'novel' produced in observation of National Novel Generation Month, computer-generated texts have innumerable forms and uses. We are already reading computer-generated texts. We are only just beginning to understand what that means.

References

Abrahams, M. (2008). Automatic Writing: Further Volumes of Philip M Parker. *The Guardian*. www.theguardian.com/education/2008/feb/05/highereducation.research1 [accessed 30 April 2018].

Ackoff, R. (1989). From Data to Wisdom. *Journal of Applied Systems Analysis*, 16(1), 3–9.

ALAMO (n.d.). *Alamo*. www.alamo.free.fr [accessed 2 October 2018].

Amazon Customer. (2004, 12 February). Review of The Official Patient's Sourcebook on Acne Rosacea, by James N. Parker M.D. *Amazon*, www.amazon.com/product-reviews/0597832129 [accessed 27 November 2016].

Anderson, B. (2006). *Imagined Communities: Reflections on the Origin and Spread of Nationalism*. London: Verso.

Anon. (1841a). From the Poughkeepsie Journal. – Hydraulic Poetry. *Green Bay Republican*, 1.

(1841b). Machine Poetry. *The Cincinnati Enquirer*, 2.

(1844). The New Patent Novel Writer. *Punch*, 6, 268.

(1845). A Latin Hexameter Machine. *The Athenæum*, 921, 621.

(1846). The Life of Wollaston. In *The British Quarterly Review*, vol. 4. London: Jacking & Walford, 81–115.

(2010). Robot with Mechanical Brain Thinks Up Story Plots (March 1931). *Modern Mechanix*. http://blog.modernmechanix.com/robot-with-mechanical-brain-thinks-up-story-plots [accessed 21 September 2017].

(2016a). Oakville A's 11U AAA (Mosquito) Outhits Vaughan in 7–3 Defeat. *GameChanger*. https://gc.com/game-57ca09c8348c02c25400003c/recap-story [accessed 24 March 2017].

(2016b). Recap Stories Now Available in the App! *GameChanger Blog*. https://blog.gc.com/2016/07/18/recap-stories-app [accessed 26 November 2016].

(2017). Majority of New Mothers in Wolverhampton Are Unmarried. *Express & Star*. www.expressandstar.com/news/local-hubs/wolver hampton/2017/11/29/majority-of-new-mothers-in-wolverhamp ton-are-unmarried [accessed 31 January 2019].

(2019). Personalizing Commentary for Credit Insurance Allocation. *Yseop*. www.yseop.com/case-studies/personalizing-commentary- for-credit-insurance-allocation [accessed 12 March 2020].

Balpe, J-P. (1995). Pour une literature informatique: Un manifeste . . . . In A. Vuillemin and M. Lenoble, eds., *Littérature et informatique: La literature générée par ordinateur*. Arras: Artois Presses Université, pp. 19–32.

Barthes, R. (1977). The Death of the Author. In S. Heath, trans., *Image, Music, Text*. London: Fontana Press, pp. 142–8.

Beer, G. (2014). The Reader as Author. *Authorship*, 3(1). http://dx.doi .org/10.21825/aj.v3i1.1066 [accessed 3 May 2017].

Boden, M. A. (2010). *Creativity and Art: Three Roads to Surprise*. Oxford: Oxford University Press.

Bök, C. (2002). The Piecemeal Bard is Deconstructed: Notes Toward a Potential Robopoetics. *Object 10: Cyberpoetics*, 10–8. www.ubu.com/ papers/object.html [accessed 28 October 2016].

Bolter, J. D. (1984). *Turing's Man: Western Culture in the Computer Age*. London: Duckworth.

(1991). *Writing Space: The Computer, Hypertext, and the History of Writing*. Hillsdale, NJ: Laurence Erlbaum Associates.

Booth, W. C. (1961). *The Rhetoric of Fiction*. Chicago: University of Chicago Press.

Borges, J. L. (1999). Pierre Menard, Author of the *Quixote*. In A. Hurley, trans., *Collected Fictions*. London: Penguin, pp. 88–95.

Bosker, B. (2013). Philip Parker's Trick For Authoring Over 1 Million Books: Don't Write. *HuffPost*. www.huffingtonpost.co.uk/entry/phi lip-parker-books_n_2648820 [accessed 30 April 2018].

Bowman, S. R., Vilnis, L., Vinyals, O., et al. (2016). Generating Sentences from a Continuous Space. In *Proceedings of the 20th SIGNLL Conference on Computational Natural Language Learning*. Berlin: Association for Computational Linguistics, pp. 10–21.

Bryson, J. J. (2018). Patiency Is Not a Virtue: the Design of Intelligent Systems and Systems of Ethics. *Ethics and Information Technology*, 20, 15–26.

BTN.com Staff. (2012). First Quarter Recap: UNLV 3, Minnesota 0. *Big Ten Network*. http://btn.com/2012/08/30/first-quarter-track-minnesota-at-unlv [accessed 16 April 2018].

(2013). Wisconsin Beats Michigan, 68–59. *Big Ten Network*. http://btn.com/2013/03/15/track-no-4-wisconsin-vs-no-5-michigan [accessed 26 November 2016].

Casebourne, I. (1996). The Grandmother Program: A Hybrid System for Automated Story Generation. In *Creativity and Cognition 1996 Conference Proceedings*. Loughborough: The Creativity and Cognition Studios, pp. 146–55.

Clarke, A. C. (2000). The Steam-Powered Word Processor. In *The Collected Stories of Arthur C. Clarke*. New York: Tom Doherty Associates, pp. 930–4 [first published in *Analog*, January 1986].

Cohen, N. (2008). He Wrote 200,000 Books (But Computers Did Some of the Work). *The New York Times*. www.nytimes.com/2008/04/14/business/media/14link.html [accessed 30 April 2018].

Cook, W. W. (1928). *Plotto: A New Method of Plot Suggestion for Writers of Creative Fiction*. Battle Creek: Ellis Publishing Company.

Cowan, S. (2012). *The Growth of Public Literacy in Eighteenth-Century England*. Unpublished doctoral thesis, University of London. https://discovery.ucl.ac.uk/id/eprint/10019999/2/__d6_Shared $_SUPP_Library_User%20Services_Circulation_Inter-Library%20Loans_IOE%20ETHOS_EThOS%20-%20Redacted%20theses_COWAN,%20S_Redacted.pdf [accessed 21 November 2020].

Dahl, R. (1954). The Great Automatic Grammatisator. In *Someone Like You*. New York: Alfred A. Knopf, pp. 250–76.

Darnton, R. (1982). What Is the History of Books? *Daedalus*, 111(3), 65–83.

Das, R., and Pavlíčková, T. (2013). Is There an Author Behind This Text? A Literary Aesthetic Driven Approach to Interactive Media. *New Media & Society*, 16(3), 381–97.

Deazley, R. (2008). Commentary on Millar v. Taylor (1769). *Primary Sources on Copyright (1450–1900)*, ed. by Lionel Bently and Martin Kretschmer. www.copyrighthistory.org/cam/tools/request/showRecord?id=commentary_uk_1769 [accessed 20 June 2019].

Dehn, N. J. (1989). *Computer Story-Writing: The Role of Reconstructive and Dynamic Memory*. New Haven: Yale University Department of Computer Science.

Dennett, D. (1971). Intentional Systems. *The Journal of Philosophy*, 68(4), 87–106.

   (1987). *The Intentional Stance*. Cambridge, MA: The MIT Press.

Dewdney, A. K. (1985). Artificial Insanity: When a Schizophrenic Program Meets a Computerized Analyst. *Scientific American*, 252(1), 10–3.

Downey, N. (2015, 8 March). Review of *The Official Patient's Sourcebook on Acne Rosacea*, by James N. Parker M.D. *Amazon*. www.amazon.com/product-reviews/0597832129 [accessed 27 November 2016].

Eisenstein, E. L. (1979). *The Printing Press as an Agent of Change*. Cambridge: Cambridge University Press.

Eureka AHRC Project. (n.d.) *Alfred Gillett Trust*. https://alfredgilletttrust.org/collections/latin-verse-machine [accessed 7 May 2019].

Eve, M. P. (2017). The Great Automatic Grammatizator: Writing, Labour, Computers. *Critical Quarterly*, 59(3), 39–54.

Febvre, L., and Martin, H-J. (1997). *The Coming of the Book: The Impact of Printing, 1450–1800*, trans. by David Gerard. London: Verso.

Fischer, K., and Bateman, J. A. (2006). Keeping the Initiative: An Empirically-Motivated Approach to Predicting User-Initiated Dialogue Contribution in HCI. In *Proceedings of the 11th Conference of the European Chapter of the Association for Computational Linguistics*. Trento: Association for Computational Linguistics, pp. 185–92.

Fish, S. (1980). *Is There a Text in This Class? The Authority of Interpretive Communities*. Cambridge, MA: Harvard University Press.

Foucault, M. (1998). What Is an Author? In J. D. Faubion, ed. and R. Hurley et al., trans., *Aesthetics, Method, and Epistemology*. New York: The New Press, pp. 205–22.

Gauchet, M. (2000). A New Age of Personality: An Essay on the Psychology of our Times. *Thesis Eleven*, 60, 23–41.

Goldschmidt, E. P. (1943). *Medieval Texts and Their First Appearance in Print*. London: The Bibliographical Society.

Goody, J., and Watt, I. (1963). The Consequences of Literacy. *Comparative Studies in Society and History*, 5(3), 304–45.

Gregory, J., and Miller, S. (1998). *Science in Public: Communication, Culture, and Credibility*. New York: Basic Books.

Hall, J. D. (2007). Popular Prosody: Spectacle and the Politics of Victorian Versification. *Nineteenth-Century Literature*, 62(2), 222–49.

(2017). *Nineteenth-Century Verse and Technology: Machines of Meter*. Cham: Palgrave Macmillan.

Hartman, C. O. (1996). *Virtual Muse: Experiments in Computer Poetry*. Hanover, NH: Wesleyan University Press.

Havelock, E. A. (1980). The Coming of Literate Communication to Western Culture. *Literacy and the Future of Print*, 30(1), 90–8.

Hayles, N. K. (2005). *My Mother Was a Computer: Digital Subjects and Literary Texts*. Chicago: University of Chicago Press.

Henrickson, L. (2018a). Computer-Generated Fiction in a Literary Lineage: Breaking the Hermeneutic Contract. *Logos*, 29(2–3), 54–63.

    (2019a). Natural Language Generation: Negotiating Text Production in Our Digital Humanity. *Proceedings of the Digital Humanities Congress 2018*. Sheffield: University of Sheffield. www.dhi.ac.uk/openbook/chapter/dhc2018-henrickson [accessed 28 February 2020].

    (2018b). Tool vs. Agent: Attributing Agency to Natural Language Generation Systems. *Digital Creativity*, 29(2–3), 182–90.

    (2019b). 'Towards a New Sociology of the Text: The Hermeneutics of Algorithmic Authorship' Empirical Studies. *Loughborough University Research Repository*. https://doi.org/10.17028/rd.lboro.c.4663709 [accessed 28 February 2020].

    (2019c). 'Towards a New Sociology of the Text: The Concept of the Author in the Digital Age' Focus Group Transcriptions. *Loughborough University Research Repository*. https://doi.org/10.17028/rd.lboro.7923944 [accessed 4 February 2020].

    (2020). Authorship in Computer-Generated Texts. *Oxford Research Encyclopedia of Literature*. https://doi.org/10.1093/acrefore/9780190201098.013.1226 [accessed 18 August 2020].

Herman, D. (2008). Narrative Theory and the Intentional Stance. *Partial Answers: Journal of Literature and the History of Ideas*, 6(2), 233–60.

Hill, W. A. (1919). *Ten Million Photoplay Plots*. Los Angeles: Feature Photodrama.

Hofstadter, D. R. (1980). *Gödel, Escher, Bach: An Eternal Golden Braid*. London: Penguin.

Houston, R. A. (1993). Literacy, Education and the Culture of Print in Enlightenment Edinburgh. *History*, 78(254), 373–92.

hugovk. (2014). 50,000 Meows. *GitHub*. https://github.com/dariusk/NaNoGenMo-2014/issues/50 [accessed 29 August 2018].

ICON Group International. (n.d.) www.icongrouponline.com [accessed 25 November 2016].

Immersive Automation. (n.d.) http://immersiveautomation.com [accessed 1 October 2017].

Johnson, D. G. (2006). Computer Systems: Moral Entities But Not Moral Agents. *Ethics and Information Technology*, 8, 195–204.

Karsdorp, F., Manjavacas, E., Burtenshaw, B., Kestemont, M., and Stokhuyzen, B. (2017). *AsiBot*. https://asibot.nl [accessed 17 December 2018].

Kazemi, D. (n.d.) NaNoGenMo. *GitHub*. https://nanogenmo.github.io [accessed 29 August 2018].

Kirschenbaum, M. (2015). What Is an @uthor? *Los Angeles Review of Books*. http://lareviewofbooks.org/essay/uthor [accessed 7 February 2015].

Klein, S., Aeschlimann, J. F., Balsiger, D. F., et al. (1973). *Automatic Novel Writing: A Status Report (Technical Report 186)*. Madison: The University of Wisconsin.

Koolhof, K. (2017). Ronald Giphart experimenteert met literaire robot. *AD. nl*. www.ad.nl/wetenschap/ronald-giphart-experimenteert-met-litera ire-robot~a5a3cb9f [accessed 1 October 2017].

Krittman, D., Matthews, P., and Glascott, M. G. (2015). Innovation Ushers in the Modern Era of Compliance. *Deloitte*. www2.deloitte.com/content/ dam/Deloitte/us/Documents/finance/us-fas-how-natural-language- is-changing-the-game-deloitte-only.pdf [accessed 15 March 2018].

Lake, R. W. (2017). Big Data, Urban Governance, and the Ontological Politics of Hyperindividualism. *Big Data & Society*. https://doi.org/ 10.1177/2053951716682537 [accessed 1 July 2019].

Latour, B. (2005). *Reassembling the Social: An Introduction to Actor-Network- Theory*. Oxford: Oxford University Press.

Lebowitz, M. (1985). Story-Telling as Planning and Learning. *Poetics*, 14, 483–502.

Lee, P. (2016). Learning From Tay's Introduction. *Official Microsoft Blog*. http://blogs.microsoft.com/blog/2016/03/25/learning-tays-intro duction [accessed 8 November 2016].

Leppänen, L., Munezero, M., Sirén-Heikel, S., Granroth-Wilding, M., & Toivonen, H. (2017). Finding and Expressing News From Structured Data. In *Proceedings of the 21st International Academic Mindtrek Conference*. Tampere: Association for Computing Machinery, pp. 174–83.

Lescure, J. (1973). La méthode S + 7 (cas particulier de la méthode M ± *n*). In *La littérature potentielle (Créations, Re-créations, Récréations*. Paris: Éditions Gallimard, pp. 143–8.

Malm, P. (2020). *The Language Effect: Why AI-Powered Copywriting Is a Marketer's (New) Best Friend*. London: Known Publishing.

Manjavacas, E., Karsdorp, F., Burtenshaw, B., and Kestemont, M. (2017). Synthetic Literature: Writing Science Fiction in a Co-Creative Process. In *Proceedings of the INLG 2017 Workshop on Computational Creativity and Natural Language Generation*. Santiago de Compostela: Association for Computational Linguistics, pp. 29–37.

McDonald, D. D. (1986). Natural Language Generation: Complexities and Techniques [internal memo]. *University of Massachusetts Department of Computer and Information Science*. Amherst: University of Massachusetts.

McGuinness, R. (2014). Meet the Robots Writing Your News Articles: The Rise of Automated Journalism. *Metro*. http://mctro.co.uk/2014/07/10/meet-the-robots-writing-your-news-articles-the-rise-of-auto mated-journalism-4792284 [accessed 30 April 2018].

McKenzie, D. F. (1999). *Bibliography and the Sociology of Texts*. Cambridge: Cambridge University Press.

McLuhan, M. (1994). *Understanding Media: The Extensions of Man*. Cambridge, MA: Massachusetts Institute of Technology.

McLuhan, M., Fiore, Q., and Agel, J. (1967). *The Medium is the Massage: An Inventory of Effects*. New York: Bantam Books.

Meehan, J. R. (1976). *The Metanovel: Writing Stories by Computer*. Unpublished Ph.D thesis, Yale University. www.semanticscholar .org/paper/The-Metanovel%3A-Writing-Stories-by-Computer-Meehan/35f03721ecef2a7315a8d85d02bacaf00660a3fb [accessed 21 November 2020].

Menabrea, L. F. (1843). Sketch of the Analytical Engine Invented by Charles Babbage, Esq. In A. A. Lovelace, trans., R. Taylor, ed., *Scientific Memoirs, Selected from the Transactions of Foreign Academies of Science and Learned Societies, and from Foreign Journals, Vol. III*. London: Richard and John E. Taylor, pp. 666–731.

Method and Apparatus for Automated Authoring and Marketing (US 7266767 B2). (2006). *Google Patents*. https://patents.google.com/ patent/US7266767 [accessed 9 October 2017].

Michael, M. (2014). How to Understand Mundane Technology: New Ways of Thinking about Human-Technology Relations. In J. R. Dakers, ed., *Defining Technological Literacy: Towards an Epistemological Framework*, 2nd ed. New York: Palgrave Macmillan, pp. 41–56.

Mittelstadt, B. D., Allo, P., Taddeo, M., Wachter, S., and Floridi, L. (2016). The Ethics of Algorithms: Mapping the Debate. *Big Data & Society*, 3(2), 1–21.

Montal, T., and Reich, Z. (2017). I, Robot. You, Journalist. Who is the Author? *Digital Journalism*, 5(7), 829–49.

Montfort, N. (2005). *Twisty Little Passages: An Approach to Interactive Fiction*. Cambridge, MA: The MIT Press.

Montfort, N., and Fedorova, N. (2012). Small-Scale Systems and Computational Creativity. In *Proceedings of the Third International Conference on Computational Creativity*. Dublin: Association for Computational Creativity, pp. 82–6.

Motta, M. (2018). The Dynamics and Political Implications of Anti-Intellectualism in the United States. *American Politics Research*, 43(3), 465–98.

Murray, S. (2018a). *The Digital Literary Sphere: Reading, Writing, and Selling Books in the Internet Era*. Baltimore: Johns Hopkins University Press.

(2018b). Reading Online: Updating the State of the Discipline. *Book History*, 21, 370–96.

Nass, C., and Moon, Y. (2000). Machines and Mindlessness: Social Responses to Computers. *Journal of Social Issues*, 56(1), 81–103.

Nass, C., Steuer, J., & Tauber, E. R. (1994). Computers are Social Actors. In *CHI '94 Proceedings of the SIGCHI Conference on Human Factors in Computing Systems*. Boston: Association for Computing Machinery, pp. 72–8.

Natale, S. (in press). *Deceitful Media*. Oxford: Oxford University Press.

National Commission on New Technological Uses of Copyrighted Works. (1979). *Final Report of the National Commission of New Technological Uses of Copyright Works*. Washington: Library of Congress.

Nehamas, A. (1986). What an Author Is. *The Journal of Philosophy*, 83(11), 685–91.

Nuttall, P. A. (1845). The Eureka. In J. Holmes Agnew (ed.), *The Eclectic Magazine of Foreign Literature, Science, and Art*. New York: Leavitt, Trow, & Co., pp. 140–1.

Parker, P. M. (2006a). *The 2007 Report on Facial Tissue Stock Excluding Toweling, Napkin, and Toilet Paper: World Market Segmentation by City*. Las Vegas: Icon Group International.

(2006b). *The 2007–2012 Outlook for Instant Chocolate Milk, Weight Control Products, Whole Milk Powder, Malted Milk Powder, and Other Dry Milk Products Shipped in Consumer Packages Weighing 3 Pounds or Less Excluding Nonfat Dry Milk and Infants' Formula in Japan*. Las Vegas: Icon Group International.

(2007). *Webster's Swedish to English Crossword Puzzles: Level 1*. Las Vegas: Icon Group International.

Parrish, A. (2015). *Our Arrival: A Novel*. http://s3.amazonaws.com/aparrish/our-arrival.pdf [accessed 29 August 2018].

Pavlíčková, T. (2013). Bringing the Author Back Into the Audience Research: A Hermeneutical Perspective on the Audience's Understanding of the Author. *The Communication Review*, 16(1–2), 31–9.

Peter, J. (1677). *Artificial Versifying | A New Way to Make Latin Verſes. Whereby Any one of Ordinary Capacity, that only knows the A.B.C. And can count 9 (though he understands not One Word of Latin, or what a Verſe means) may be plainly taught (and in as little time, as this is reading over) how to make Thouſands of Hexameter and Pentameter Verſes which ſhall be True Latine & True Verſe, and Good Senſe.*, 2nd ed. London: Kings-Head at Sweetings-Alley end, next House to the Royal Exchange in Corn-hill.

Pinch, T. J., and Bijker, W. E. (1984). The Social Construction of Facts and Artefacts: Or How the Sociology of Science and the Sociology of Technology Might Benefit Each Other. *Social Studies of Science*, 14, 399–441.

Podolny, S. (2015). If an Algorithm Wrote This, How Would You Even Know? *The New York Times*. www.nytimes.com/2015/03/08/opinion/sunday/if-an-algorithm-wrote-this-how-would-you-even-know.html [accessed 30 April 2018].

Polti, G. (1895). *Les trente-six situations dramatiques*. Paris: Mercure de France.

Portela, M. (2018). Writing under Constraint of the Regime of Computation. In J. Tabbi, ed., *The Bloomsbury Handbook of Electronic Literature*. London: Bloomsbury, pp. 181–200.

Powers, T. M. (2013). On the Moral Agency of Computers. *Topoi*, 32(2), 227–36.

Prescott, T. J. (2017). Robots Are Not Just Tools. *Connection Science*, 29(2), 142–9.

Racter [Chamberlain, W., and Etter, T.]. (1984). *The Policeman's Beard Is Half Constructed*. New York: Warner Software/Warner Books.

Radford, A., Wu, J., Amodei, D., et al. (2019). Better Language Models and Their Implications. *OpenAI*. https://openai.com/blog/better-language-models [accessed 20 August 2020].

Ray Murray, P., and Squires, C. (2013). The Digital Publishing Communications Circuit. *Book 2.0*, 3(1), 3–23.

Reeves, B., and Nass, C. (1996). *The Media Equation: How People Treat Computers, Television, and New Media Like Real People and Places*. Cambridge: Cambridge University Press.

Regan, D. (2015). The Cover of *The Sun Also Rises*. *GitHub*. http://alsorises.org [accessed 29 August 2018].

Roberts, S. (2017). Christopher Strachey's Nineteen-Fifties Love Machine. *The New Yorker*. www.newyorker.com/tech/annals-of-technology/christopher-stracheys-nineteen-fifties-love-machine [accessed 11 March 2019].

Ryan, J. (2017). Grimes' Fairy Tales: A 1960s Story Generator. In *Interactive Storytelling: 10th International Conference on Interactive Digital Storytelling*. Cham: Springer, pp. 89–103.

Saenger, P. (1999). Reading in the Later Middle Ages. In G. Cavallo and R. Chartier, eds., L. G. Cochrane, trans., *A History of Reading in the West*. Cambridge: Polity Press, pp. 120–48.

Schoff Curtin, R. (2017). The Transactional Origins of Authors' Copyright. *The Columbia Journal of Law and the Arts*, 40(2), 175–235.

Searle, J. R. (1980). Minds, Brains, and Programs. *The Behavioral and Brain Sciences*, 3(3) 417–57.

Shillingsburg, P. L. (2006). *From Gutenberg to Google: Electronic Representations of Literary Texts*. Cambridge: Cambridge University Press.

Skains, R. L. (2019). *Digital Authorship*. Cambridge: Cambridge University Press.

Smiggy. (2002, 19 December). Follow Your Nose, Couldn't Put It Down! [Customer Review]. Review of The 2007 Report on Facial Tissue Stock Excluding Toweling, Napkin, and Toilet Paper: World Market Segmentation by City, by Philip M. Parker. *Amazon*. www.amazon.co .uk/gp/customer-reviews/RCNPTIBJJNAQV [accessed 30 April 2018].

Spence, P. R., Edwards, A., Edwards, C., and Jin, X. (2019). 'The Bot Predicted Rain, Grab an Umbrella': Few Perceived Differences in Communication Quality of a Weather Twitterbot Versus Professional and Amateur Meteorologists. *Behaviour & Information Technology*, 38(1), 101–9.

Stahl, B. C. (2004). Information, Ethics, and Computers: The Problem of Autonomous Moral Agents. *Minds and Machines*, 14(1), 67–83.

Tang, J., Yang, Y., Carton, S., Zhang, M., and Mei, Q. (2016). Context-Aware Natural Language Generation with Recurrent Neural Networks. *Cornell University Library (arXiv)* https://arxiv.org/abs/ 1611.09900 [accessed 25 June 2017].

Teigen, P. M. (1987). A Prolegomenon to the Interpretation of *The Printing Press as an Agent of Change*. In P. F. McNally, ed., *The Advent of Printing: Historians of Science Respond to Elizabeth Eisenstein's* The Printing Press as an Agent of Change. Montreal: McGill University, pp. 8–14.

Tenen, D. (2017). *Plain Text: The Poetics of Computation*. Stanford: Stanford University Press.

Tomasula, S. (2018). Our Tools Make Us (and Our Literature) Post. In J. Tabbi, ed., *The Bloomsbury Handbook of Electronic Literature*. London: Bloomsbury, pp. 39–58.

Turner, S. R. (1993). *MINSTREL: A Computer Model of Creativity and Storytelling*. Unpublished doctoral thesis, University of California Los Angeles. www.semanticscholar.org/paper/Minstrel%3A-a-compu

ter-model-of-creativity-and-Turner/745b24c90f089339f7e9e2209d4a cebfb2f1ec82 [accessed 21 November 2020].

Urbs Media. (n.d.). www.urbsmedia.com [accessed 25 February 2018].

Valtteri (n.d.) [archived by *Internet Archive*]. https://web.archive.org/web/20190120010217/https://www.vaalibotti.fi [accessed 18 August 2020].

van der Weel, A. (2001). The Communications Circuit Revisited. *Jaarboek voor Nederlandse boekgeschiedenis*, 8, 13–25.

(2011a). *Changing Our Textual Minds: Towards a Digital Order of Knowledge.* Manchester: Manchester University Press.

(2011b). Our Textual Future. *Logos*, 22(3), 44–52.

(2014). From an Ownership to an Access Economy of Publishing. *Logos*, 25(2), 39–46.

(2015). Appropriation: Towards a Sociotechnical History of Authorship. *Authorship*, 4(2). https://doi.org/10.21825/aj.v4i2.1438 [accessed 1 July 2019].

Vuillemin, A., and Lenoble M., eds. (1995). *Littérature et informatique: La literature générée par ordinateur.* Arras: Artois Presses Université.

Weizenbaum, J. (1966). ELIZA – A Computer Program for the Study of Natural Language Communication Between Man and Machine. *Communications of the ACM*, 9(1), 36–45.

Whalen, Z. (2018a). A Python Script that Writes 800-page Children's Books. *Zach Whalen*. www.zachwhalen.net/posts/a-python-script-that-writes-800-page-childrens-books [accessed 30 August 2018].

(2018b). *The Several Houses of Brian, Spencer, Liam, Victoria, Brayden, Vincent, and Alex. GitHub.* https://github.com/zachwhalen/nngm17 [accessed 28 August 2018].

(2019). The Many Authors of The Several Houses of Brian, Spencer, Liam, Victoria, Brayden, Vincent, and Alex: Authorship, Agency, and Appropriation. *Journal of Creative Writing Studies*, 4(1) https://scholarworks.rit.edu/jcws/vol4/iss1/6. [accessed 20 July 2020].

Wiener, N. (1950). *The Human Use of Human Beings: Cybernetics and Society*. London: Eyre and Spottiswoode.

Wilson, A. (2004). Foucault on the 'Question of the Author': A Critical Exegesis. *The Modern Language Review*, 99(2), 339–63.

Winograd, T. (1971). *Procedures as a Representation for Data in a Computer Program for Understanding Natural Language*. Unpublished doctoral thesis, Massachusetts Institute of Technology. https://dspace.mit.edu/handle/1721.1/7095 [accessed 21 November 2020].

Acknowledgements

This Element would hardly have been possible without the guidance and insight of, among many others: Drs Wim Van Mierlo, Clare Hutton, Simone Natale, and Laura Dietz, as well as Professors Adriaan van der Weel and Jenny Fry. Thanks are also due to Loughborough University's Digital Humanities Research Group and the Martin Hall crew. For the less sexy but more comprehensive version of this book (i.e. my doctoral thesis), see https://doi.org/10.26174/thesis.lboro.10596404.

Cambridge Elements ≡

Publishing and Book Culture

SERIES EDITOR

Samantha Rayner
University College London

Samantha Rayner is a Reader in UCL's Department of
Information Studies. She is also Director of UCL's Centre for
Publishing, co-Director of the Bloomsbury CHAPTER
(Communication History, Authorship, Publishing, Textual
Editing and Reading) and co-editor of the Academic Book of
the Future BOOC (Book as Open Online Content) with UCL
Press.

ASSOCIATE EDITOR

Leah Tether
University of Bristol

Leah Tether is Professor of Medieval Literature and Publishing
at the University of Bristol. With an academic background in
medieval French and English literature and a professional
background in trade publishing, Leah has combined her
expertise and developed an international research profile in
book and publishing history from manuscript to digital.

ABOUT THE SERIES

This series aims to fill the demand for easily accessible, quality texts available for teaching and research in the diverse and dynamic fields of Publishing and Book Culture. Rigorously researched and peer-reviewed Elements will be published under themes, or 'Gatherings'. These Elements should be the first check point for researchers or students working on that area of publishing and book trade history and practice: we hope that, situated so logically at Cambridge University Press, where academic publishing in the UK began, it will develop to create an unrivalled space where these histories and practices can be investigated and preserved.

Cambridge Elements ☰

Publishing and Book Culture
Digital Literary Culture

Gathering Editor: Laura Dietz
Laura Dietz is a Senior Lecturer in Writing and Publishing in
the Cambridge School of Creative Industries at Anglia Ruskin
University. She writes novels and studies novels, publishing
fiction alongside research on topics such as e-novel readership,
the digital short story, online literary magazines, and the
changing definition of authorship in the digital era.

ELEMENTS IN THE GATHERING

The Network Turn: Changing Perspectives in the Humanities
Ruth Ahnert, Sebastian E. Ahnert, Catherine Nicole Coleman and Scott
B. Weingart

Reading Computer-Generated Texts
Leah Henrickson

A full series listing is available at: www.cambridge.org/EPBC

Printed in the United States
by Baker & Taylor Publisher Services